THE JEWISH QUARTERLY

The Jewish Quarterly is published four times a year
by The Jewish Quarterly Pty Ltd

Publisher: Morry Schwartz

ISBN 9781760645472 E-ISBN 9781743824368
ISSN 0449010X E-ISSN 23262516

Subscriptions 1 year print & digital (4 issues): £42 GBP | $56 USD | $74.99 AUD
1 year digital only: £25 GBP | $32 USD | $44.99 AUD. Payment may be made
by Mastercard or Visa. Includes postage and handling.

Subscribe online at jewishquarterly.com or email subscribe@jewishquarterly.com
Correspondence should be addressed to: The Editor, The Jewish Quarterly,
22–24 Northumberland Street, Collingwood VIC 3066 Australia
Phone +61 3 9486 0288 Email enquiries@jewishquarterly.com

The Jewish Quarterly is published under licence from the
Jewish Literary Trust Limited, which exercises a governance function.

UK Company Number: 01189861. UK Charity Commission Number: 268589.

Issue 262, November 2025

THE JEWISH QUARTERLY

Gaza
and the Jews

A history

Tom Segev is an award-winning Israeli historian and journalist whose books include *One Palestine, Complete*, *The Seventh Million* and *A State at Any Cost: The Life of David Ben-Gurion*.

Ira Moskowitz is a translator and editor based in Modi'in, Israel.

The Jewish Quarterly is grateful for support from:

The Anglo–Jewish Association

The Exilarch's Foundation

The Polonsky Foundaton

Gaza and the Jews

A history

Tom Segev
(translated by Ira Moskowitz)

Introduction

In the early seventeenth century, a revered rabbi living in the city of Gaza became famous for the hundreds of liturgical poems he composed, usually set to Turkish, Arab or Spanish folk melodies. At least one of these songs, *Ya Ribbon Olam*, is still popular today, primarily sung around the dining table on Sabbath eve. Rabbi Israel Najara was the scion of a family that once lived in the city of Nájera in northern Spain. Following the expulsion of Jews from Spain in 1492, the family had made its way to the Land of Israel.

One of his poems was recently uncovered by the Israeli researcher Tova Beeri and published during the war that erupted in the wake of Hamas's invasion of Israel on October 7, 2023. It was written as a song of praise for the Jews residing in Gaza: "God loves you," Najara assured them. He described them as righteous and generous people, and beseeched God on their behalf: "Give them life, peace in their homes." But, over the centuries, peace was not to be their customary fate in a city that lived from one conquest to the next. The name of Gaza is recorded in the military annals of some of the most illustrious imperial commanders, including Alexander the Great, Richard the Lionheart, Saladin and Napoleon Bonaparte. When Winston Churchill visited Gaza in 1921 in his role as colonial secretary, the city was still in ruins – the aftermath of its conquest by the British Army at the end of World War I.

Conquerors mainly sought to control Gaza because of its strategic and commercial location, on the sea route leading northwards along the Levantine coast from Egypt, and with roads leading eastwards from it towards Damascus, and from the Arabian Peninsula to the Mediterranean Sea. As the city changed hands, its residents were often massacred or sold into slavery; if they were lucky, they were only expelled. The city was completely destroyed more than once, but it rose again time after time – until the next conqueror appeared on the scene. Gaza's thousands of years of history have been shaped as much by religious beliefs, desires and passions as by rational imperial interests – even more so, at times. The Jews of the city lived this dynamic: they resided in Gaza as long as it appeared that Najara's prayer found divine favour. When war erupted, they fled the city; when the situation improved, they returned. They also grappled with the debate in Jewish law on whether Gaza was part of the Land of Israel, and hence whether they should follow the rules that apply to Jews living in foreign lands. In any case, during the millennium of Jewish presence in Gaza, its Jews seldom developed a deep sense of local patriotism.

Jewish pilgrims and traders who passed through Gaza on their way from Egypt to the Levant often wrote of enjoying their time in the city. Obadiah of Bertinoro (Italy), a rabbi known for his commentary on the Mishnah, arrived in Gaza in 1488 and wrote about a local rabbi who insisted that he spend the Sabbath at his home. "We drank seven or eight cups before eating and we were happy," Obadiah recounted. Like many tourists, he was taken to see some stone columns that were purportedly the remains of the building that mighty Samson had brought crashing down upon the Philistines.

"Gaza is a very beautiful city," a Jewish merchant from the Crimean Peninsula declared in the early nineteenth century, describing a vibrant and colourful urban atmosphere, with stores, cafés and bathhouses. Of course, it was not always like this. A Russian Jewish

A revolutionary spiritual message burst forth from Gaza and suddenly shook the entire Jewish world

immigrant in the late nineteenth century complained: "Its streets are narrow and winding, as in all the cities of antiquity. The houses are dark and built in a chaotic way." Others grumbled about the filth and stench that made it hard to breathe. Hordes of Arab urchins dressed in rags swarmed around every visitor, begging for alms or a piece of bread. David Ben-Gurion, the future prime minister of Israel, witnessed this when returning from his service as a soldier in the British Army at the end of World War I. "Children surround the train with outstretched arms, shouting that they're impoverished and begging for handouts," he wrote in his diary. The minutes from an Israeli cabinet meeting in October 1956 record an unforgettable statement that Ben-Gurion made about Gaza: "If I believed in miracles, I'd wish for it to be swallowed up by the sea." Years later, many continue to identify with this wish.

The Jews enjoyed periods of stability in Gaza, with synagogues, a school, a cemetery and a judicial system led by a rabbi and lay officials. Most of them engaged in commerce, artisanry and agriculture, as well as the production and sale of wine; some served as agents in commercial transactions with Egypt and even with Europe. It seems that the cost of living was lower in Gaza than in other cities in the Southern Levant. The Jews were usually a small minority that wielded little influence, but in the seventeenth century a revolutionary spiritual message burst forth from Gaza and suddenly shook the entire Jewish world. Nothing could be compared to it – until the days of the Reform movement and secular Zionism. It was here, in Gaza, that the seeds were planted for the three conflicts that make it so difficult to create a shared Jewish identity, especially in Israel: religious versus secular Jews, Mizrahi versus Ashkenazi Jews, and Jews versus Arabs.

1. Conquest and exile

I will send down fire upon the wall of Gaza.

Over the years, there have been many attempts to calculate the Jewish population of the Southern Levant in ancient times. This has involved, in part, identifying Jewish settlements and measuring the extent of the agricultural lands they may have cultivated. The statistical conclusions from very limited demographic data, including biblical references, are at best estimates. Naturally, scholars are not in agreement about these estimates, which today increasingly rely on AI applications. The numbers generally range from several tens of thousands to a million Jews – and some say even more. At certain periods, the Jews were a majority in the Land of Israel, but never in Gaza.

The Bible mentions Gaza about twenty times. According to the Book of Genesis, it was originally earmarked for one of Noah's descendants sometime after the flood. In the plan to divvy up the land, which was apparently formulated several centuries after the Exodus from Egypt as recounted in the Bible, Gaza was assigned to the Tribe of Judah. Indeed, the Book of Judges (1:18) tells us that Judah captured the city and its territory. But the next verse explains that Judah was unable to establish control in Gaza because the Philistine enemy was equipped with iron chariots. The Philistines came mainly from the western part of the Mediterranean and were later called the "sea peoples". Several biblical references (for example, Amos 9:7, Jeremiah 47:4) cite Crete (Caphtor) as the homeland of the Philistines. Gaza was one of the areas they conquered.

This conquest occurred around 1330–1200 BCE. The Twelve Tribes of Israel may have already arrived in the Promised Land. The biblical account of the period of the forefathers and the Kingdom of Israel is primarily a religious-literary rendering from the first millennium BCE, long after the events it describes. Some researchers accept the biblical story as truth, as do millions of believers – Jews, Christians and Muslims. Others, including Israeli researchers, reject the historical value of the story almost entirely, mainly due to the lack of archaeological evidence to support it. This includes the story that, according to the biblical narrative, occurred forty years after the Exodus from Egypt: the conquest of Canaan under the leadership of Joshua ben Nun.

We can assume that the Israelites gradually settled in Canaan, eventually forming the Kingdom of Saul, the first king of Israel. Scholars estimate that he ruled between 1025 and 1005 BCE. Ongoing battles against the Philistines took place during his reign, but he was unable to conquer Gaza. It is written (II Samuel 8:1) that King David defeated the Philistines, but the city is not mentioned among his conquests. The First Book of Kings states that King Solomon ruled over all the kingdoms "from the river [Euphrates] to the land of the Philistines and to the border with Egypt" (4:21). Gaza is not mentioned by name here. A few verses later, however, the text states that he "ruled over the whole region west of the river, from Tiphsah to Gaza" (4:24). The word "to" leaves room to question whether he also ruled in Gaza itself. Indeed, the Bible's compilers often placed this word before the name Gaza, making it difficult to determine whether the reference includes the city or only the area to its borders. Later, the Second Book of Kings reports (18:8) that Hezekiah, king of Judah, "struck down the Philistines as far as Gaza and its border areas, from watchtower to fortified city". The phrase "to fortified city" was then a commonly used expression meaning vast territories and did not refer to a specific geographic location.

The repeated mention of the city reflects emotional, religious and national longings and not only concrete interests. This is exemplified in two mythological figures: Samson, a coveter of women, and David, a teenage shepherd who defeated the giant Goliath. The Philistines are portrayed as a bitter, perennial enemy. At one point, God punished the Israelites for their sinful behaviour by subjecting them to Philistine rule for forty years (Judges 13:1). Several prophets in the Bible invoked curses of doom upon the Philistines. The prophet Amos, speaking in the voice of God, declared: "I will send down fire upon the wall of Gaza and it will devour its fortresses" (Amos 1:7). Jeremiah, Zephaniah and Zechariah made similar prophecies. Indeed, the armies of Assyria, Babylonia and Persia unleashed such fire on Gaza and the entire land.

In the eighth century BCE, Tiglath-Pilser III, king of Assyria, captured Gaza from the Philistines and turned it into a vassal state. He refrained from annexing it to

Less than fifty years later, the next empire marched into the Levant

his empire, presumably in order to maintain the city's standing as a centre of commerce. Nebuchadnezzar II, king of the Babylonians, conquered the Levant in the early seventh century BCE as part of his campaign to destroy the Assyrian Empire. In 586 BCE, the Temple in Jerusalem was set ablaze, the city was razed and tens of thousands of Jews were exiled to Babylon. The Jews who managed to remain in the country were described as the "surviving remnant".

Less than fifty years later, the next empire marched into the Levant. The new Persian ruler, King Cyrus, permitted the Jews to return from exile in Babylonia and even to build a new temple. The Persians ruled for two centuries until Alexander the Great arrived on the scene in 332 BCE. This was another one of the tragic chapters that shaped the chronicle of Gaza: its people resisted the invasion and Alexander laid siege to the city for months. According to contemporaneous battle reports, his army also deployed sophisticated mechanical equipment unlike anything used by other armies at the time. In late October 332 BCE, its infantry – under the command of Alexander himself – managed to infiltrate the city. As expected, the residents of Gaza were brutally punished, as was customary in those days: the men were executed, while the women and children were sold into bondage. It is estimated that the conquest of Gaza claimed the lives of about 10,000 civilians. Alexander and his army then continued towards Egypt.

According to some assessments, Jews constituted the largest religious group in the area at that time, their number swelling to 2 million or more with the return of Jews from their Babylonian exile. Most of them engaged in agriculture.

Antiochus Epiphanes, one of the rulers of the Seleucid Empire formed after the death of Alexander the Great, rose to power in 175 BCE and imposed a series of religious prohibitions on the Jews. This sparked a rebellion and ultimately led to Jewish political independence under the leadership of the Hasmonean dynasty. Jonathan Apphus, the brother of the revolt's leader, Judah the Maccabee, came close to conquering Gaza. According to the First Book of Maccabees, his troops besieged Gaza, set fire to its surrounding fields and villages, and took plunder. The people of Gaza then "pleaded for peace and Jonathan agreed to make peace with them" (11:62). This suggests that he did not conquer Gaza, but settled instead for a capitulation agreement. Another account, subject to some dispute, claims that Jonathan's brother Simon captured the city and brought Jews to live there.

Whatever the case, Gaza experienced a wave of immigration from Greece during that period and Greek language and culture came to dominate the city's life for the next half-century. Jewish entrepreneurs and traders also came to the city to participate in its commercial boom. The Jerusalem Talmud mentions Gaza as one of the central marketplaces where Jews purchased homes, fields, slaves and maidservants. Around the year 100 BCE, however, Alexander Yannai, a notoriously brutal Hasmonean king, imposed a long siege on Gaza and ultimately ordered its destruction.

About forty years later, the Levant was captured by the Romans. One of the first decisions of the Roman occupation regime was to rebuild Gaza in a new location, about 4 kilometres south of its previous site. The city would be accorded the exceptional status of a semi-autonomous entity operating under the province of Syria, and its rebuilding was assigned to Syria's Roman governor, Aulus Gabinius, a controversial general and politician described as frivolous and dissolute. He sought to weaken the influence of the Hasmoneans and thus wanted the new city of Gaza to be populated with as few Jews as possible. This was an inauspicious start to the relations between the Jews and the Romans. Later came uprisings that ended in gruesome failure, claiming the lives of hundreds of thousands of Jews and culminating in the destruction of the Second Temple in 70 CE. During the Great Jewish Revolt, as it is commonly called, rebel forces also attacked Gaza. The Jewish historian

Josephus reports that "many villages [in the vicinity of Gaza] were pillaged, and immense numbers of inhabitants were captured and slaughtered" (The *War of the Jews* II 18:457).

The Great Jewish Revolt failed, as did another rebellion nearly seventy years later, this time led by Simon Bar Kochba. It occurred during the reign of Emperor Hadrian, a ruler depicted by many historians as enlightened and progressive, though in Jewish history he is considered one of the most hostile oppressors. Under his rule, a new city was built upon the ruins of the Temple in Jerusalem. The name given to the city – Aelia Capitolina – pays tribute to Hadrian (Aelia is part of his full name), as well as to the god Jupiter and two associated Roman deities that together formed the Capitoline Triad. Hadrian's efforts to extinguish Jewish identity included a prohibition on Jews entering Aelia Capitolina, except on the day marking the destruction of the Second Temple.

The revolt led by Bar Kochba began in the autumn of 131 (or in the following spring) and continued for about three and a half years. Archaeologists have found a network of tunnels secretly prepared by the rebels before they mounted their offensive in the Gaza area. Nearly a thousand villages were destroyed, and some estimates say that as many as 580,000 Jews were killed during the revolt – more than 4000 in the city of Gaza – not including those who died from hunger and plagues. Various sources report that tens of thousands of Jews were sold into bondage. Jewish captives were brought to the slave market in the city; some were sold on the spot and others were taken to be sold in Egypt. A later source reports that the glut in the market drove down the price of a Jewish slave to below that of a horse.

In the years that followed, the Roman authorities imposed increasingly oppressive measures against the Jews. Hadrian is particularly loathed by the political right in Israel today for officially changing the name of the province of Judea to Syria Palaestina. All this was aimed at reducing the Jews in the province from a majority to a minority.

The prohibition on entering Aelia Capitolina, formerly Jerusalem, led Jews to settle in other cities. Gaza came to be viewed as a substitute for the destroyed temple and Jews flocked to it instead of making a pilgrimage to Jerusalem. As an ancient manuscript states: "And they came from the four corners of the land to Tiberias and to Gaza to see the temple." Gaza was later described as a "holy city", attracting people driven by "a longing for holiness", and sites were

Gaza was home to several famous philosophers, and to theatres, circuses and even a school for rhetoric

established in the city "for reading and prayer at any time". Security arrangements were required, as the need "to station guards at night" is noted. One of the sources emphasises that pilgrims to Gaza came from the west – presumably referring to Egypt, North Africa and perhaps Yemen. Emperor Antoninus, the adopted son of Hadrian and his heir, meanwhile repealed the last of the anti-Jewish laws, including the prohibition on visiting Aelia Capitolina. He visited Gaza at least once and upon his return to Rome told of the luxury and splendour he found there.

The spread of the Christian faith in Rome brought to Syria Palaestina a series of governors who were hostile towards Jews. They instituted policies of discrimination and persecution, including capital punishment for Jews who married Christians or circumcised their Christian slaves. The prohibition on visiting Jerusalem was reinstated during the Byzantine period. Despite these difficulties, and perhaps in part as a response to them, the Mishnah and Talmud – the two most important Jewish works since the Bible – were written during the ensuing centuries. Most of the Talmud's sages lived in the Galilee but at least two resided in Gaza. The Jerusalem Talmud notes the beauty of the city, and in later sources Gaza is portrayed as an international hub, flourishing both culturally and economically. It was home to several famous philosophers, and to theatres, circuses and even a school for rhetoric, which, historical research suggests, numbered Jews among its students. The Jews also benefited from the economic prosperity in the area and built the largest synagogue in the Land of Israel to date.

2. City of ambiguity

It is agreed in Gaza that [Jews] should not go to the sea later
[in the week] than Wednesday.

In the mid-1960s, Egyptian archaeologists announced the discovery of the remains of a very large church on Gaza's coastline. The church, dated to the fifth century, featured two beautiful mosaics depicting animals, "a holy figure playing a lyre" and an inscription in Hebrew and Greek. The Egyptian publication included photographs that led Israeli archaeologists to claim almost immediately that it was in fact a synagogue rather than a church, and that the lyre player was none other than King David, as spelled out in the inscription above his head. No crosses appear in the mosaic. After Israel captured the Gaza Strip in the 1967 Six-Day War, a systematic excavation was conducted in cooperation with the Israeli military government. The researchers had to address a number of questions, including why such a small community needed such a huge synagogue, though the city's Jewish population did grow from time to time. In the mosaic, King David is modelled after the Greek mythic hero Orpheus, dressed like a Byzantine emperor and crowned with a diadem. A lion cub, a giraffe and a snake surround the king, listening to him play the lyre. Similar images have been found at various sites, not necessarily Jewish, in Europe. While David's name is written in Hebrew letters, its spelling does not follow the convention established with the dissemination of the First Book of Samuel.

The second of the two mosaics is adorned with grape vines and olive branches, which also appear elsewhere as Jewish symbols. The branches form circles around several animals: a lioness suckling her cub, another giraffe, peacocks, a leopard, a bear, a zebra and more. The Greek inscription embedded in the mosaic floor notes the Hebrew names of two brothers: "We, Menachem and Yeshua, sons of the late Yishay, wood merchants, as a sign of respect for a most holy place, donated this mosaic." The local calendar date is noted, which archaeologists have calculated to correspond to the year 508. Israeli researchers argue that this date proves that the building could not have been a church because depictions of this type were banned from churches by the Byzantines in the year 427. The representation of David in the floor mosaic reflects a liberal interpretation of the Second Commandment's prohibition on making "any graven image, or any likeness of what is in the heavens above, or on the earth below, or in the waters under the earth". Human figures also appear in mosaics found later in other synagogues. The remains of a workshop that produced the tiles for the mosaics were found near the site; it presumably supplied tesserae for both synagogues and churches. It is not clear when, why and how the magnificent synagogue was destroyed.

Several Jews from the city tried to memorialise themselves: their names – and sometimes their longings as Jews – are etched into stone at various locations. But who they actually were as real, flesh-and-blood people, no one can say. The question will remain an eternal, sad enigma. Such is the fate of a man named David ben Joseph Zvi. His name was carved into a marble column discovered in the Great Mosque of Gaza in the early 1880s. The column is over 3 metres high, with a circumference of about 60 centimetres. Two circles were also etched into the column, with a Hebrew inscription inside one of them: "May the angel who has redeemed me from all harm grant me the privilege to go up to Jerusalem." The first part of the sentence is taken from Jacob's blessing on his sons in the Book of Genesis (48:16). Nothing more is known about David ben Joseph Zvi and archaeologists have been unable to date the column definitively. It may be from the Roman, or even the Greek, period; perhaps it indicates the existence of a synagogue – perhaps not. Thus, as often happens in archaeological excavations, the focus turns to the circumstances of the artefact's discovery and its subsequent history. One of the first Zionist settlers in Ottoman Palestine, Zvi Hirschfeld, learnt that the column was in the possession of two priests and purchased it from them. When Hirschfeld died, the historic column was placed on his grave in the old cemetery in Rishon LeZion, a city about 15 kilometres south of Tel Aviv, and it can still be seen there today.

The identity of Hananiya bar Yaakov, whose name was also etched into one of the columns in the Great Mosque of Gaza, is likewise shrouded in mystery. Perhaps the column had once stood in a synagogue. In any case, the community evidently sought to honour the man, since his name is adorned with a seven-branched menorah that has a shofar on one side and an etrog on the other, all surrounded by a large bouquet

The Great Mosque of Gaza was destroyed during the war that erupted in October 2023

of leaves and fruits. Israeli researchers have hypothesised that the honoured personage was the benefactor who funded the construction of the synagogue – just as the wood merchants who funded the David mosaic were memorialised. About a hundred years after its discovery, the inscription was defaced during the First Intifada. The Great Mosque of Gaza was destroyed during the war that erupted in October 2023.

In the eighth and ninth centuries, the Jewish community in Gaza was sufficiently well established to commission the work of Masoretic scribes and scholars who engaged in preserving the precise traditional wording of the Bible and other Jewish sacred writings. The names of some Gazan Jews, their way of life and their community structure have been revealed in the centuries-long and still unresolved debate on Gaza's status – that is, whether it is considered part of the Land of Israel. Several verses in the Book of Joshua (for example, 13:3) suggest that Gaza is indeed part of Canaan and thus worthy of acquisition in the course of any potential conquest of the entire land. However, in referring to Goliath the Philistine, the Book of Joshua notes that there were no *Anakim* (a race of giants) among the Israelites as there were in Gaza: "No Anakim were left in the land of the people of Israel; only in Gaza, in Gath and in Ashdod did some remain" (11:22). Long before the magnificent synagogue was built in Gaza, the Jews in the city asked the community in Caesarea to send them a *dayan* (rabbinic judge). The fact that there was no local dayan indicates that the Jewish community in Gaza was still small, and the request it sent to Caesarea reflects its wish to grow. The Jerusalem Talmud recounts that the community in Caesarea sent a well-known dayan named Isaac ben Nahman, but only on "loan" – that is, on condition that he would not permanently settle in Gaza. According to Jewish law, the holiness of the Land of Israel is such that a Jew is not allowed to leave it permanently, and the Jews of Caesarea apparently considered Gaza a "foreign city".

The conundrum in Jewish law stems from the notion that the sanctity of the territory conquered in the days of Joshua – which included Gaza – expired when the Jews were exiled to Babylonia and the First Temple was destroyed. Later, when Cyrus, king of Persia, permitted them to return, the newly settled land acquired a "second sanctification" – but Gaza lay outside the new borders of holiness. This question of sanctity sparked political conflicts, including a struggle for power among Jewish leaders, while also determining the ways of life of individual Jews.

One of the leaders of the Egyptian Jewish community, a man named David ben Daniel, argued that Ashkelon and Gaza did not belong to the Land of Israel, entitling him to include these "foreign" cities in his jurisdiction. The counterargument was that the Jews of Gaza did not observe the second day of Jewish festivals as is customary in foreign lands, thus proving that the "first sanctification" applied to Gaza. A resident of Gaza by the name of Mevorach ben Nathan travelled to Egypt to retrieve his brother's remains for burial in the Land of Israel. As his brother's heir, he also planned to take his possessions – but several leaders of the community in Egypt contended that he did not have rightful claim to all his brother's property. However, the sages of Gaza ruled in his favour; in a detailed letter they sent to Fustat, the first capital of Egypt under Muslim rule, they rebutted a potential claim that their ruling carried less weight than that of Egypt's sages by identifying themselves as being "displaced" to Gaza. That is, they were residents of the Land of Israel who had relocated to Gaza, presumably under duress. Their letter, written on a scroll in Hebrew block letters, eventually fell into the hands of the Austrian imperial family and is preserved today in the Papyrus Museum at the Austrian National Library in Vienna. It was not a statement of claim: the fifteen sages of Gaza who signed the letter as supplicants made their plea to Fustat for a true and just ruling. There is no record of how the authorities in Fustat responded.

The ambiguity of Gaza's status sometimes allowed its Jews to choose the judicial authority most favourable to them. In the fifteenth century, they turned to the chief rabbi of Egypt, David ben Solomon ibn Zimra (known as the "Radbaz"). One of the members of the community died, leaving two wives whose respective marriage contracts were not identical, which raised the question of how to divide his property. The Radbaz ruled that Gaza was indeed outside the bounds of the Land of Israel. Consequently, when Gazan Jews sought an exemption from the mandatory tithes on produce grown in the Land of Israel, they again turned to the rabbi of Egypt.

One of the merchants in Gaza sought the counsel of Rabbi Joseph di Trani (known as the "Maharit"), who lived in Safed. The merchant's problem was that his wife was refusing to return to Gaza from Egypt. She had asked to flee Gaza, ostensibly in fear of an impending epidemic, but her husband, suspecting this was just an excuse to leave, conditioned his consent on her taking only enough clothes for a short stay in Egypt. After she left, he discovered that she had taken all her belongings. When he demanded that she return, his wife refused. The question was whether he could force her to come back; this was possible in the Land of Israel. The case demanded a ruling based on principle. The embittered husband may have turned to the Maharit not only as one of the leading rabbis of his generation, but also as a resident of Safed rather than Egypt. Presumably, the husband figured that the rabbi would consider Gaza part of the Land of Israel from the perspective of Jewish law. But the Maharit did not fulfil the husband's expectation: he ruled that the borders demarcated at the return from Babylonian exile, rather than those of Joshua's conquest, now applied. The former did not include Gaza, so from the perspective of Jewish law it was not part of the Land of Israel. Over the years, countless rabbis and sages challenged this ruling, each offering his own interpretation.

Rabbi Levi ben Habib (the "Ralbach"), who served as chief rabbi in Jerusalem for two decades in the sixteenth century, detected a separatist tendency among the Jews of Gaza that also permeated religious customs, such as the reading of the Book of Esther on Purim. "I asked about the tradition of Gaza, and they told me that it was a completely new tradition," he disapprovingly noted. The Jews of Gaza sometimes even formulated local laws for themselves, such as restrictions on going to the seashore: "It is agreed in Gaza that [Jews] should not go to the sea later [in the week] than Wednesday as it is liable to lead to the violation of the Sabbath."

> *"I asked about the tradition of Gaza, and they told me that it was a completely new tradition"*

The question of whether Gaza is part of the Land of Israel has been raised in almost every generation. Jewish religious settlers who came to live in the Gaza Strip after it was captured in the Six-Day War discussed this question, as have some far-right Israelis who plan to settle in Gaza after expelling its Palestinian residents.

Meanwhile, a fascinating theory put forward in Israel suggests that not all biblical references to Gaza relate to the city we know today. An ultra-Orthodox Jewish researcher named Israel Shapira has written: "In a number of places in the Bible, the city of Gaza is mentioned in a manner that, given the context, is very difficult to reconcile with the Gaza we know in the southern part of the land of the Philistines." He suggests that the Bible may be referring to a city in the West Bank whose original name was also Gaza. Indeed, other countries also have more than one city with the same name.

3. Remote outpost

Do not approach anyone while wearing shoes and do not speak with anyone without sitting and tucking your legs beneath you.

Until forced to leave Gaza about twenty years before the birth of the State of Israel, Jews had lived almost continuously in the city for about 1300 years as a minority among Muslims. It is not easy to piece together the story of the Levant's conquest by "the Arabs" – the medley of tribes that mobilised behind Mohammed in the first half of the seventh century. The end of the Byzantine period was marked by corruption, decay and economic crisis. The burden of taxation was unbearable, land remained in the hands of the few, and many farmers became impoverished city dwellers. One of the authors of the Talmud is reputed to have said: "A man without land is not a man." Entire Jewish communities ceased to exist, and many Jews left the country. It is estimated that, at the beginning of the Muslim era, up to 25,000 people lived in Gaza and its surrounds, but with only a few hundred Jews among them. The fanaticism of Byzantine Christianity had stirred hatred by humiliating and persecuting followers of other religions. Consequently, the Muslims were generally welcomed by Gaza's Jews as the successors to the Byzantine rulers. In the initial stages of the Islamic conquest, the Muslims treated Jews more favourably than they did Christians and they also lifted the ban on Jews visiting Jerusalem.

Yet the attitude of the Muslim authorities towards the local population varied from dynasty to dynasty. As Islamic rule became more deeply entrenched, the Qur'an – and its definition of Jews as foreign and inferior – took on greater weight. Jews were ordered to demolish synagogues they had built in the early Islamic period, special taxes were imposed on them and they were forbidden to ride in carriages. Jews were required to distinguish themselves by wearing items such as a black turban or a pendant in the shape of a calf. At one stage, they were forced to post figurines of Satan on the doors of their homes. Jews were also forbidden to hire Muslim servants and one Muslim ruler declared that Jews could only be employed in finance or medicine. At times, some of these regulations were revoked, depending on the mood and whims of the particular ruler. The Seljuk dynasty, which sprang from Muslim nomads in Central Asia, was notoriously murderous. Their brutality sparked revolts by the residents of Jaffa and Gaza, which were repressed in rivers of blood. Gaza was defeated by the Seljuks in 1078; its residents were executed and it took two generations to recover. Meanwhile, the Crusaders arrived.

Nearly 200 years of Crusader rule in parts of the Holy Land also left a legacy of horrific violence, especially in Jerusalem. The First Crusade reached the outskirts of Gaza, but the Crusaders refrained from immediately entering the city, perhaps because they figured it was not worth the effort: Gaza still lay in ruins after being destroyed by the Seljuks. For about fifty years, it served purely as a military stronghold. Then, a church was built, perhaps as part of an initiative by King Baldwin III to revive the city. Saladin restored Gaza to Muslim hands and Richard the Lionheart tried unsuccessfully to recapture it. Based on the detailed accounts made by Jewish pilgrims from Europe travelling to or from Egypt, it seems there were no Jews living in Gaza during the Crusader era. Benjamin of Tudela, a Jewish merchant and geographer from Spain who set off on his travels in 1165 and only returned eight years later, makes no mention of Gaza. Another Jewish traveller and chronicler, Petachia of Regensburg (Germany), visited the area around the same time and likewise makes no mention of Gaza. Perhaps the city was not open to visitors during its period as a military stronghold, or it was simply not considered worth visiting. Judah Alharizi, a well-known Jewish poet and translator from Spain, arrived in Gaza via Egypt in 1218, stayed for a while and mentioned the city in one of his poems – though only in the context of his difficult journey: "We offered praise to God with tambourine and dance – for enduring on our way through the desert sands." It is safe to assume that if Alharizi had spent time with Jews in Gaza, he would have made note of it. The expulsion of the Crusaders by the Mamluks and the return of Muslim rule enabled Jews to return to Gaza, though the region was in deep decline. In the transition of power from the Crusaders to the Mamluks, some 120,000 residents of the Holy Land – mostly Christians – either fled or were killed, and the population shrank to about 300,000.

The Mamluks were an elite military force composed of soldier-slaves, primarily of Turkish-Caucasian origin, who were taken to Egypt in their youth and forced to convert to Islam. They crushed the Crusader Kingdom of Jerusalem but feared that the Christians might try to return. To prevent this, the Mamluks set out to systematically destroy cities and ports in the Holy Land. The coastal region became a bleak wasteland, its residents replaced by nomadic shepherds. However, just as the prohibition on visiting Jerusalem had served to

According to Gucci's account, the Jews of Gaza made and exported good wines

strengthen the Jewish population in Gaza, the city now benefited from the Mamluks' destruction of the coastal cities: Gaza suffered the least damage and even absorbed a wave of Jews who had been expelled from France.

Christian travellers to the Holy Land perhaps encountered Jews more often than in their home countries, which might explain why they note repeatedly that they met "many Jews". Giorgio Gucci, a city councilman and wool trader from Florence, was sent to the Holy Land in 1384 by King Charles III of Naples, tasked with assessing the feasibility of launching a new crusade. Gucci spent some time in Gaza. He praised the climate and noted the abundance of delicious food, bread, meat, chickens and eggs, and the plentiful grapevines in the area. According to his account, the Jews made and exported good wines – a real compliment coming from an Italian traveller. It appears that the Jews of Gaza enjoyed a near monopoly in this trade, as they were exempt from Islam's prohibition on winemaking.

A French nobleman, Ogier IX d'Anglure, spent time in Gaza in 1395 and noted that members of different religions in the city could be identified by the coloured stripes on their head coverings: white for Muslims, indigo blue for Christians, yellow for Jews and pale pink for Samaritans – a group claiming to be descendants of the tribes of Israel. Felix Fabri, a Dominican friar from Switzerland who visited the Holy Land twice in the 1480s, composed a tourist guide-book that included lodging recommendations and prices, as well as warnings against the deceitful antics of local merchants. He recommended the bathhouses in Gaza because the Jews were not allowed there. Christians were permitted to enter because, unlike the Jews, "their body does not give off a foul odour," Fabri explained.

A famous traveller from Germany, Arnold von Harff, wrote that during a visit in 1499 the Jews in Gaza turned the local police against him. According to his account, Jews informed on him when he pretended to be a merchant in order to pay a lower transit fee; pilgrims were required to pay a higher sum. He was detained for three weeks in a local prison and issued a warning to future pilgrims upon his release: "Beware of the Jews' deceitfulness." On the other hand, a German traveller by the name of Martin von Baumgarten praised the Jewish interpreter he hired in Gaza, around the year

1507. The interpreter, David, advised him to purchase Muslim attire so that he could roam the city safely.

In time, the travelogues became more informative, yielding data on the Jewish population in various areas: 300 families in Safed, 150–250 in Jerusalem, seventy in Gaza, twenty in Hebron, and so on. The numbers are not consistent in the different reports that have survived, and there is no way of verifying them. Still, some of the travel journals make for fascinating reading. One such example is a book written by the Florentine banker Meshulam ben Menachem, the scion of an affluent Jewish family from Volterra in Tuscany. He set off for Jerusalem via Egypt in the summer of 1481, apparently fulfilling a vow he had made during a time of distress. Even today, his book is considered an important source on the life of Jews in the Holy Land at that time. Before reaching Gaza, he was delayed at Khan Yunis by reports of Arab marauders in the area. "We heard that Arabs were in the land and that no one was venturing outside his home," he wrote. The reports said that three people had been robbed and murdered. He later wrote a long and detailed guide, advising travellers on what they should and should not do on the always-perilous journey to Gaza. It was not only that bandits and local tribes attacked the convoys from Egypt to rob the passengers, Meshulam explained; they were also driven by hatred for non-believers from Europe – Christians and Jews alike – who did not behave fittingly in their eyes. Therefore, it was essential always to dress appropriately and act respectfully: "Even when you need to relieve yourself, make sure not to pull up your clothing," he warned. "Even when you urinate, bend towards the ground until your organ is three fingers from the ground and then relieve yourself, because if a single drop falls on your legs or clothing, they say you are impure and need to take a stone and scratch yourself with it, or wash it with water immediately. And do not approach anyone while wearing shoes and do not speak with anyone without sitting and tucking your legs beneath you."

Once he finally reached Gaza, Meshulam received a warm welcome, which he fully appreciated after ten days of riding in the Sinai Desert in the July heat. He described the city as "a good land whose fruits are excellent", even though, as he put it, the wine was produced by Jews. He made a practice of noting the number of Jews living in the places he visited and his information on the Jewish community in Gaza – fifty to sixty families – may be the first reliable estimate of its size. Most lived on "Jews' Street" in the upper part of the city, the site of "Delilah's house, where the mighty Samson dwelled". They had a small and beautiful synagogue, and engaged in various types of artisanry, as well as farming and the production of oils. Some years later, a loosely woven fabric – gauze – was developed in Gaza and exported to Europe for medical use. Indeed, its name in European languages may derive from its city of origin.

Meshulam mentions two Jews he meets in Gaza: Rabbi Moses ben Yehuda Sefardi and his father-in-law, a goldsmith. Sefardi was an esteemed member of the community, though Meshulam describes him as "a bit slow of speech". Rabbi Obadiah of Bertinoro, who visited Gaza seven years later, wrote about a night of drinking with a local rabbi, Solomon of Prague, and noted that he was popular with the community's elders and leaders. Obadiah also described the arduous journey across the desert, though he experienced easier conditions than Meshulam, travelling in April and mostly at night. He learnt that the city's Jewish community comprised seventy families at the time.

Here, then, is a glance at a small Jewish community, feeling isolated in a tough and remote city. The Jews, who had their own internal disputes, generally lived in peace with their Arab neighbours, though they were often vulnerable to the consequences of violent conflicts among the Arabs themselves. Meshulam was an eyewitness to the particularly brutal execution of an Arab thief that triggered bloody clashes in the city. If there were forbidden romantic liaisons between Jews and Arabs, neither community spoke about it; perhaps it was only later that such liaisons occurred. This question sparked curiosity in the wake of the war that erupted

Gaza was about to enter a new era as part of a dramatic sequence of events that swept the Levant

in October 2023 when Jewish genetic markers were found in the unidentified corpses of some Hamas members, suggesting that they may have been the descendants of Jews who had converted to Islam.

Meshulam did not cite the total number of residents in the city, only saying that they were "more than the sand on the seashore". He was likely referring to the large number of travellers who arrived in Gaza and had to wait until it was possible to continue their journey. Exiting the city sometimes required complex security operations, with convoys of no less than 4000 people. Sometimes it was necessary to wait until a group of 7000 people gathered, along with 10,000 camels. According to Meshulam, the authorities took measures to secure the northward journey, working in cooperation with the governors of Ramla and Jaffa to kill thousands of Arab bandits.

Meshulam may not have realised that he was describing a historical twilight period: Gaza was about to enter a new era as part of a dramatic sequence of events that swept the Levant, the Jewish people and humanity at large. The harassment of Jews in Spain, which had already prompted some of them to immigrate to the Holy Land, came to a climax on 31 March 1492, when all Jews were ordered to either convert to Christianity or leave Spain. The Jews of Portugal were soon presented with the same choice. The Jewish community in Gaza again benefited from these travails, as documented by Yitzhak Ben-Zvi, drawing on Ottoman archival records in Istanbul. According to Ben-Zvi, who went on to become Israel's second president, about 5000 people lived in Gaza in 1525, including ninety-five tax-paying Jewish families. Eight years later, the number of Jewish families had grown slightly to ninety-eight, and by 1550 had risen to 116 (plus five single men). Meanwhile, a new conqueror had arrived: in 1517, the Mamluks were defeated and replaced by the Ottomans, whose rule was to last for nearly 400 years.

4. The Ottomans

He used his time in the city to test his vision of Jewish independence.

The Ottoman Empire had become a great power while the Mamluk Sultanate had sunken into decay and corruption, like empires that had come before – and as the Ottoman Empire would in due course.

Several cities, including Gaza under the Mamluks, tried to fend off the troops of Sultan Selim I but were quickly and brutally subdued. Most of the Jews welcomed the new conquerors: many of those expelled from Spain had found refuge in Ottoman lands and the Jews in Palestine had reason to believe that their lot would also improve under Ottoman rule. Some even saw the Ottoman conquest as a harbinger of messianic redemption. According to a census conducted by the new regime, the entire population in the Southern Levant numbered about 300,000 and included over 10,000 Jews. The numbers fluctuated over the years – and this was also true of Gaza.

Under the Ottomans, Jews were designated a protected people in accordance with the rules of Islam, which gave rise to various restrictions and regulations. Some had already been in force during the Mamluk period, such as a special tax, and the requirement for Jews to wear a piece of yellow fabric and to hang a small bell on their necks when entering a bathhouse. The construction of new synagogues was prohibited. These regulations were revoked from time to time, or replaced by others – sometimes more severe, sometimes more lenient. Still, the new regime generally allowed the Jews to conduct their lives autonomously. While not permitted to establish a central authority, they were able to maintain a religious and communal status quo that included a recognised rabbinical court in Jerusalem. In time, most of the Jews living in the Southern Levant were exiles from Spain who spoke Ladino; the second generation of the Spanish diaspora also identified with this cultural heritage. Many Jews used Arabic as a spoken language, sometimes using Hebrew letters to write in what they called Judeo-Arabic.

Jews lived in Gaza primarily because the city was less expensive or offered promising commercial opportunities. Nearly all the city's Jews considered two conditions essential for Jewish life in Gaza: personal safety and access to basic religious institutions such as a synagogue and rabbinate. From time to time, renowned rabbis took up residence in Gaza, including Jacob Berab and his student, Joseph Karo, the compiler of the foundational Jewish legal code, the *Shulchan Aruch* (first printed in 1565). Berab noted that the judges who sat in the Jewish court in Gaza were no less meritorious than those in Jerusalem. Another distinguished rabbi who lived in Gaza for a number of years was Eliezer bar Arhah, author of about fifty books. Nonetheless, it seems that many Jews did not feel at home in the city, instead usually finding that their sense of belonging was rooted in their family and neighbourhood. According to a new study by the Israeli historian Yuval Ben-Bassat, the same could be said for the city's Arab residents.

Most of the Muslims were cordial towards the Jewish minority in Gaza, according to Mordechai Elkayam, one of the sons of the community's leader, Nissim Elkayam. Wealthy Arabs boasted about buying only kosher meat, and the butchers competed to hire the services of the *shochet* (religious slaughterer). Bedouin customers from the area purchased food products and clothing from Jews and paid in grain, sheep and wool. The Jewish merchants usually had horses, mules, donkeys or camels. During the summer months, some of them went to live with the Bedouins, leaving their families behind in the city and dressing and living according to their hosts' customs; an outsider could not have distinguished between the Bedouins and their

Jewish guests. In this way, the Jews learnt to speak the Bedouin dialect, which was different from the Arabic spoken by the city dwellers or local farmers. In the evenings, they regaled each other with stories and fables, jokes and riddles, and recited rhymes and poems.

Some Jewish merchants gave the Bedouin grain producers a partial payment in advance, paying the rest at harvest time, when they received the produce. Wheat was sold at the city market, while barley was mainly exported to Europe. Some of the Jews employed peasant farmers and Bedouins, including women, for the harvest of so-called "bitter apples" (colocynth), a cross between a squash and a watermelon. The bitter fruit was in demand in Germany and England as a remedy for digestive ailments and assorted pains.

> *Many residents of Gaza were illiterate and sought the Jews' assistance in writing letters and petitions to the authorities*

Many residents of Gaza, Bedouins and city dwellers alike, were illiterate and sought the Jews' assistance in writing letters and petitions to the authorities. "In this way, the Jews became an essential asset among the population that needed this [service] and paid well for it," noted Mordechai Elkayam.

When conducting business in the city, the Jews wore European clothing and a tarbush. The economic stability ushered in by the new government boosted the scope of activity at the Gaza port and its commercial importance. Jewish community leaders tried to encourage immigration to the city. One such effort involved a merchant from Jerusalem named David Cohen Elsafadi, who passed through the city of Gaza on a business trip to Egypt. The leaders of the city's Jewish community proposed that he and his wife relocate to Gaza and offered him a generous tax exemption. As a seasoned merchant, he asked for a sworn commitment, and he received a commitment from the community leaders but not a formal oath. Five years later they saw less value in his presence in Gaza and rescinded his tax exemption. When he took his case to the city's rabbi, Isaac Shalom ben Arhah, who also had relocated from Safed to Gaza, he was given a ruling in his favour.

As in the past, some Jews arrived in Gaza as refugees from other cities, including Safed, Tiberias and even Jerusalem, whose Ottoman governor, Muhammad ibn Farrukh, was harsh in his treatment of the Jewish community. A convoy of twenty residents, most of them women and children, defied a prohibition on leaving Jerusalem and tried to flee to Gaza. They were caught and handed over to the authorities. Other Jews arrived in Gaza after fleeing from earthquakes or outbreaks of disease, and some came from overseas. There were also Jews who left Gaza, presumably for reasons of comfort or profit, or for family reasons. Letters written by some of them reflect a culture of emigrant longings and even a sense of loyalty towards their former city. One letter writer, Ephraim ben Shemariah, was still a youngster when his parents left Gaza for Egypt. They prospered in their new homeland, becoming wealthy perfume merchants. Ephraim was an outstanding student who went on to head the rabbinical court in Fustat and was later appointed chief rabbi of Egypt. Feeling a deep connection with Gaza, he closely followed what was happening there and became one of its prominent patrons. Perhaps he also felt obliged, as a prominent citizen of Egypt, to help the community in Gaza. The need for monetary support from Jews living outside the Holy Land created an entire class of fundraising emissaries who passed through Gaza when travelling to and from other countries. Their activity created a kind of international "buzz" that perhaps helped attract a fascinating character to the city: David Reubeni. Regarded by some as a visionary and by others as a delusional charlatan, he brought to Gaza a fantasy of establishing an independent Jewish state in the Land of Israel.

The year was 1522. Reubeni travelled, probably by boat, back and forth to Alexandria, staying for a few days in Gaza each time. He sometimes presented himself as David, the son of King Solomon. It appears that he used his time in the city to test his vision of Jewish independence on the people he met. At the same time he boasted of his wide network of connections, both Jews and non-Jews. "They love me, and I love them," he declared. One of the people he spoke with in Gaza, a man named Abraham, complained about the way the Muslims treated Jews: "They hate us and prefer dogs to us." Reubeni consoled him with messianic tidings: "Have no fear because the end is coming soon. The Holy One brings down the evil ones and raises up the downtrodden, and you will soon see great things and much confusion and conflicts between kings." Reubeni promised that when this happened, he would take Abraham on a tour of the Temple. He imagined a military-diplomatic campaign that would echo across the world, all the way to America. In the meantime, he prayed with the Jews of Gaza. He ate dinner on Sabbath eve at the home of the richest Jew in the city, Rabbi Daniel, "an esteemed and devout" man, in Reubeni's words. As midnight approached, his host shared a personal problem with him: His son was "a handsome man of valour", but members of the community complained that he led a life of debauchery. Reubeni promised to apply his almost unlimited powers of persuasion on Daniel's son, who indeed then vowed to mend his ways. The next day, the community paid for Reubeni's passage back to Alexandria.

Many researchers have tried to understand this man, apparently without complete success and without reaching a consensus: He remains a charming enigma. Wikipedia describes him as "a mysterious Jewish 'half-mystic, half-adventurer'" and the Hebrew version of Wikipedia adds that he was a "statesman". No one is certain where he was born; various theories propose Spain, North Africa, the Arabian Peninsula, India or Afghanistan as his birthplace, while another hypothesis identifies him as an Ethiopian Jew. In 1524, two years after his visits to Gaza, he arrived in Venice and asked the city's Jews to organise an audience for him with Pope Clement VII. Somehow this was arranged and Reubeni proposed a Jewish-Christian military alliance to seize the Holy Land from the Turkish sultan and establish Jewish independence. The pope provided him with letters to present to the king of Portugal and the emperor of Ethiopia. King João III of Portugal met with Reubeni several times and, according to Reubeni, promised to supply him with eight warships. The king then changed his mind and ordered Reubeni to leave Portugal, fearing that he was conspiring to convert Christians to Judaism. Reubeni returned to Italy and sought to present his strategic fantasy to Charles V, emperor of the Holy Roman Empire.

The emperor's advisors determined that he was an unhinged swindler and expelled him. Undeterred, he made another attempt to win an audience with the emperor and was then arrested, tried by the court of the Inquisition and executed in 1538 – perhaps hanged, perhaps burned at the stake.

Reubeni was often asked whether he regarded himself as a prophet or a messiah, and he responded that he was neither a prophet nor the son of a prophet. He was merely a minister of war and the son of King Solomon, from the seed of David ben Yishai. Today, there are streets named for him in Jerusalem, Tel Aviv and several other Israeli cities. Over a hundred years after his death, a prophet and a messiah would indeed rise to prominence in Gaza. For a time, the two men turned the city into a sort of metropolis of spiritual awakening and reform. No other city surpassed Gaza in this regard, not even Jerusalem.

5. Messianic tidings

His name and the name of Gaza ... were tarnished with a connotation of heresy and charlatanism.

It all started in the autumn of 1660 when a wealthy Jew from Damascus, Samuel Lisbona, settled in Gaza. His family name indicates that he had arrived in Damascus from Portugal, via Italy. Like a number of other merchants in Damascus, he decided to leave when the Ottoman authorities imposed steeper taxes. Gaza, meanwhile, continued to extend a welcome to businessmen, including Jews, who wished to make a home in the city with their families. Lisbona also hoped to find his daughter a husband in Gaza. It was not going to be easy, since the young woman suffered a defect in one of her eyes; according to another account, she had only one eye.

In his distress, Lisbona travelled to Jerusalem to ask Rabbi Jacob Hagiz to recommend a suitable match for his daughter. The rabbi pointed him towards one of his most brilliant students: Nathan ben Elisha Haim Halevi Ashkenazi. At the time, Jerusalem was a small city and did not serve as a centre of government. Its population of 5000–10,000 people included 1000–2000 Jews, most of them crowded into a shared quarter. The tall stone wall encircling the city gave it a heightened sense of security but also created an atmosphere of claustrophobia.

When he was a boy, Nathan's father, a native of Germany or Austria, travelled several times at the community's behest to solicit donations from affluent Jews in North Africa and Europe. His father's overseas experiences presumably piqued Nathan's interest in the wider world. On one trip, his father took several religious manuscripts to a printing press in Venice, and Nathan came to appreciate the propaganda potential of this relatively new technology, which even then enabled a type of mass communication.

Rabbi Hagiz studied the Kabbalah, Jewish mystical teachings in the spirit of Rabbi Isaac Luria (the "Ari"), who lived in Safed in the sixteenth century. Hagiz was also interested in mathematics, philosophy, astronomy and medicine, and his yeshiva students studied Spanish as a foreign language. Thus, unlike most of his peers in Jerusalem, Nathan grew up with a view of the modern world and the Renaissance. When he was twenty, he married Lisbona's daughter and moved to her home city, Gaza. From this point, it is customary to refer to him as Nathan of Gaza.

His wealthy father-in-law did not push him to make a living and the clever, shrewd and imaginative young man, who tended to succumb to his emotions, started to take an interest in all sorts of magic and miracles, and to delve into the mysteries of the Kabbalah. In the course of this pursuit, he engaged in "repairing souls" – exposing the hidden sins of people and telling them how to "repair" their lives. Perhaps he was doing the genuine work of a psychological counsellor or perhaps he was simply a wily imposter – or some combination of the two. It is also possible that he truly believed in his spiritual power to help people. In any case, more and more people fell under his sway and came to view him as a man of God and aprophet. He was regarded as more than just a fortune teller, rather as someone who could see into people's hearts and reveal their innermost secrets. He prescribed stringent fasts and all sorts of asceticism, which he also took upon himself.

Reports of Nathan as a man of God spread beyond Gaza and reached Egypt, where they stirred the interest of one of the community's leaders, a banker named Raphael Joseph. He sent his brother and some of his men to Gaza to assess the reputed prophet's true nature. The brother came home with an unequivocal answer: Nathan of Gaza was indeed a man of God. It was the beginning of a beautiful friendship in which Raphael Joseph would finance a large part of Nathan's enterprise. Staying at Joseph's home at the time was Shabtai Zvi, an emissary of the Jewish community in Jerusalem who had come to solicit funds. It is puzzling that the leaders of the Jewish community in Jerusalem had selected him as their fundraiser: he was already known as an eccentric, though it was only later – when he was suspected of pocketing some of the money he had collected – that he acquired the reputation of a swindler.

Shabtai Zvi was born in 1626 in Ottoman Izmir to a family of Greek origin, the middle child of a successful and learned businessman. His first name notes the fact that he was born on the Jewish Sabbath. He received a religious education and completed his studies successfully. The story of his life is full of question marks and should be treated with scepticism: many of the accounts are sexual in nature, beginning with the abuse he was said to have suffered when he was just six years old. Perhaps this trauma gave rise to his self-image as the messiah. He married three times, and there are also rumours concerning his impotence and asceticism, as well as exhibitionism and all sorts of other uncontrollable urges. All this and more have spurred many attempts to decipher his psychological makeup, passions and weaknesses, including an inclination to isolate himself, symptoms of bipolar disorder and, most of all, a strong impulse to place himself at the centre of scandals. In Izmir, he embarrassed his two brothers when he started to pronounce the explicit name of God in public, in violation of one of the most sacred rules of Judaism. Some suspected and feared that he sought to establish a religious cult, maybe even a new religion, perhaps a sort of Christian offshoot. On one occasion, he bought a large fish, placed it in a baby carriage and wheeled it through the city's alleyways. This odd behaviour was also embarrassing in light of the elevated status of his father, who served for a time as the chief rabbi of Rhodes. Shabtai Zvi's brothers sent him to Salonika and to Egypt, where his third marriage took place, to a woman who was also the subject of salacious gossip. Finally, at the age of thirty-six, he moved to Jerusalem.

Nathan of Gaza was seventeen years younger than Shabtai Zvi. We can assume that he and his Jerusalemite friends were familiar with the neighbourhood lunatic who sequestered himself in his room or wandered off to the desert and holy sites outside the city – sometimes completely naked, often accompanied by a servant, bursting into song and calling out the explicit name of God. He even climbed a hill and attempted to stop the sun in its course, as Joshua ben Nun had once done, according to the biblical narrative. Youngsters mocked Shabtai

> *Nathan announced that the visitor had a very "lofty soul" and was in fact God's messiah*

Zvi, and perhaps Nathan was one of them. It appears that the two men's personal acquaintance began when Shabtai Zvi, on his way to or from Egypt, stopped in Gaza in order to meet the famous prophet Nathan and to seek solace for his tortured soul. Nathan received him and announced that the visitor had a very "lofty soul" that was in no need of repair because he was in fact God's messiah. Shabtai Zvi had already declared this, yet it is unlikely that anyone had taken him seriously. At this stage the matter seems to have remained a private discussion. The sensational public announcement that he was the long-awaited messiah only came later. And when it did, the masses believed it.

Nathan of Gaza later claimed that he had immediately recognised Shabtai Zvi when they met in Gaza, because an angel from heaven had already revealed to him in a dream that Shabtai Zvi was God's messiah. Nathan of Gaza was determined to convince his community to believe his story. He had always spoken truthfully and had never lied, he wrote, explaining that during his encounter with the angel, he had been in a state of ecstasy that continued unabated for twenty-four hours. In his dream, a chariot had passed before him with the image of Shabtai Zvi etched on its side, just as the image of Jacob is said to be etched on God's throne. The would-be messiah eagerly went along with all of this. Some contend that he exploited Nathan of Gaza to cultivate his status as the messiah, and some even portray the would-be prophet as his loyal subordinate. It is reasonable to assume that each took advantage of the other. And it is possible, of course, that at least one of them believed in the messianic mission. Perhaps they both believed in each other. The leading Israeli scholar of the Kabbalah, Gershom Scholem, wrote that Shabtai Zvi himself was a "miserable leader", with no plan of action or ability to derive any benefit from his hallucinations and maladies. Nathan of Gaza, on the other hand, was driven by Shabtai Zvi's paradoxical personality to promote Sabbateanism, as the messianic movement he founded in Gaza came to be known. However, it is also possible that what really happened is most aptly described on the website of the ANU Museum of the Jewish People in Tel Aviv:

Nathan of Gaza ... wrote, produced and directed the greatest film about messianic Judaism in the modern era ... The rumour took wing and the buzz surrounding the new messiah grew with his road trips and visits to Jewish communities. Nathan's missives attended this hysteria and the real euphoria that pervaded Diaspora Jewry.

The small community in Gaza received Shabtai Zvi as one of its cherished sons. Rabbi Moshe Najara, who inherited his position from his grandfather, the liturgical poet, gave the would-be messiah his blessing. He could claim that he was acting in the spirit of his grandfather, who had also allowed himself a bit of mischief that offended the conservative establishment. In his poem for the Shavuot festival, "My Beloved Went Down to His Garden", Israel Najara depicts God as a bridegroom and the people of Israel as a bride: "My beloved went down to the garden, to his spice beds, to make love with the nobleman's daughter." The poem created an uproar. "He permitted himself to say to God, blessed be He, everything that adulterers say to each other," an eminent Jerusalem rabbi wrote in disgust. The poet's grandson encouraged people to believe in Shabtai Zvi and many flocked to him, which also attracted the attention of Muslims.

The Ottoman Empire, which generally treated Jews with greater tolerance than was accorded to them in most of Christian Europe, initially showed lenient indifference towards Sabbateanism. When necessary, Nathan of Gaza paid off whoever needed to be placated. The Qadi of Jerusalem allowed Shabtai Zvi to ride through the streets of the city on a horse, despite the law forbidding Jews from doing so. But the authorities could no longer ignore the massive support he garnered, particularly in light of the opposition that arose among the rabbis of the religious establishment in Jerusalem and elsewhere. Shabtai Zvi rejected or changed a number of customs and rules, including some of the fast days mandated by Jewish law. The rabbinate's leaders saw him as a loathsome non-believer and competitor, and strived to prove that he was not the messiah, just a charlatan and dangerous subversive. The rabbis finally persuaded the Ottoman authorities to expel him from the country.

At this stage, Shabtai Zvi's messianic tidings reflected a political message that could be perceived as rebellious: his admirers described him as a king, or even as "the king of kings" (which in the Jewish liturgy refers to God). Indeed, he dressed like a real king when riding his horse. They addressed him as "our master, our teacher – may his glory be exalted", a Hebrew honorific whose acronym ("AMIRAH") could be misheard by Muslims as "emir", the Arabic word for the Ottoman governor or ruler. Some of his followers revised the wording of the Jewish prayer expressing loyalty to the authorities ("He who grants salvation to kings"), replacing the name of the Ottoman sultan with Shabtai Zvi's name. Indeed, he had promised them that the sultan himself would one day restore the Land of Israel to the Jews and crown him king. Some of his devotees began using a new calendar that began with the advent of the messiah, Shabtai Zvi. His decision to cancel the fast commemorating the Temple's destruction was accompanied by a plan to renew sacrifices on the Temple Mount, which had been a sacred site for Islam for nearly a millennium. Foreign diplomats began to report on his activity.

Traditional Judaism expresses a longing for the return of the Jewish people from exile, saying this will occur when the messiah appears as ordained by God – perhaps following a tectonic disaster of biblical proportions. Shabtai Zvi spoke about the end of exile and a return to the Land of Israel as an impending event and mission, especially in the wake of the expulsions from Spain and Portugal and the pogroms in Eastern Europe. These events intensified the mass longing for redemption. In various countries, mainly in Europe, thousands (and some say tens of thousands) of people who had abandoned their Jewish identity now openly embraced it. Some even went back to using the Hebrew language. A growing number of Jews began to consider immigrating to the Land of Israel.

Centuries later, some scholars identified Shabtai Zvi's teachings as an early incarnation of political Zionism

A rumour of a miraculous return to Zion by flying on clouds led some people to climb onto rooftops, spread their arms to the skies – and crash to the ground. The Ottoman authorities feared a mass migration of Jews to the Land of Israel, and this was one of the reasons they acceded to the request to expel Shabtai Zvi. Upon his expulsion, he set off for cities in the Ottoman Empire and Western Europe. Everywhere he went, he warned his audience not to act like the people of Jerusalem who had expelled their king and brought God's curse upon themselves. Nathan of Gaza declared that Jerusalem had forfeited its sanctity by expelling Shabtai Zvi and that Gaza had become the new seat of holiness.

Centuries later, some scholars identified Shabtai Zvi's teachings as an early incarnation of political Zionism and saw Theodor Herzl as one of his successors. Herzl made a point of rejecting this parallel in his diary. In any case, at the time there was a deep political and ideological rift around the world between Jews who followed messianic Sabbateanism and their conservative opponents. The need for a messianic message had been evident in the past, and it would arise again after the demise of Sabbateanism. However, to this day, Sabbateanism remains unparalleled in the professional and imaginative promotion of Jewish messianism.

Nathan of Gaza did not accompany Shabtai Zvi on his travels in Europe, yet he orchestrated his activities on a daily basis from his home in Gaza. Nathan was very experienced in transferring funds, familiar with every ruse and ploy; he took care of everything – travel tickets, visas, accommodation and so on – and managed Shabtai Zvi's schedule of meetings and appearances. There was a steady stream of letters, instructions and invitations sent via messengers travelling on horseback, by camel or by ship. Nathan of Gaza controlled Shabtai Zvi like a puppet on a string. New means of communication fired Nathan's imagination, just as, centuries later, the internet would fire the imaginations of those discovering its wonders for the first time. He often had to coach Shabtai Zvi on what to say and what not to say, and how to extract himself from the various embarrassing situations in which he found himself, having transgressed the laws of the lands he visited. The self-proclaimed messiah even got into violent confrontations with his Jewish opponents. In Izmir, he came to pray in the synagogue but found the service too long for his taste, so he went with a group of his followers to another synagogue. But the members of the second synagogue were fearful of him and blocked his entrance. He called for an axe and started to hack away at the door until they opened it for him.

Nathan's mission of PR man and producer in Gaza became more and more difficult because, at a certain stage, it seems that Shabtai Zvi's status as God's messiah was no longer enough for him and he began to wonder openly whether he himself was divine. He began to imagine his soul's intimate relationship with God as part of the very essence of God. In this, he was apparently influenced by various Christian ideas.

Public attention focused on his spiritual message, but what began in Gaza as a religious and political dispute evolved into a conflict between conservatism and social reform. Shabtai Zvi's gospel from Gaza, for example, included a truly revolutionary message: Jewish feminism. Female "prophets" began to appear in different places in the Holy Land, spreading his messianic teachings. In some synagogues, women were allowed to be "called up" to recite blessings over the Torah. Moreover, Shabtai Zvi preached full gender equality: "Oh you poor women. Because of Eve's sin, you give birth in sorrow and are enslaved to your husbands and everything you do depends on their consent. Happy are you that I came into the world to make you free and happy like your husbands, because I came to erase the sin of Adam."

His Jewish opponents in Germany, Italy, Holland and other lands endeavoured to portray him as subversive. Many feared that

Sabbateanism would undermine their own status vis-à-vis the rulers of their countries of residence.

Meanwhile, in Gaza, Shabtai Zvi did his utmost to prevent or at least slow the unravelling of his project. But he was unsuccessful. The would-be prophet was brought for questioning before the sultan's council in Adrianople, now Edirne in Turkey, and given a choice: conversion to Islam or death. He chose to convert. It is hard to exaggerate the trauma this caused among his shocked followers.

Nathan of Gaza, while also shocked, courageously remained steadfast. He declared that he had not lost faith in his messiah and quickly set off to meet with him. But it was too late to save the movement. Some Jews followed Shabtai Zvi's lead and converted to Islam, while most of his supporters abandoned him. His name and the name of Gaza, which until then had evoked messianism and the word of God, were tarnished with a connotation of heresy and charlatanism.

Unfortunately, there is no full record of what Shabtai Zvi and Nathan of Gaza said to each other when they met in Adrianople in 1669. Neither ever returned to Gaza. Shabtai Zvi died in 1676 at the age of fifty; Nathan of Gaza died about four years later, aged thirty-seven. In a letter to the Jews of his beloved city, Nathan of Gaza promised them eternal life as a reward for their support for the messiah, and he envisioned Gaza absorbing thousands of Jews after the resurrection of the dead. In conclusion, he returned to one of the word games he and Shabtai Zvi were fond of: by detaching the final letter of the Hebrew word for "Gaza", two words are produced, meaning "mighty God". The two men were buried somewhere in the Balkans, perhaps in Montenegro. But as befits the secrecy and mystery that were central to their identity, their graves have never been found. According to various reports, tiny clandestine cells of Sabbateanism survived in various places around the world.

The well-known Israeli columnist Jacky Levy described Shabtai Zvi as a rock star whom everyone wants to forget, and despite the many academic studies, his story is perhaps the least known of the formative narratives in Israeli culture. The level of enmity and anger his name evokes to this day varies in correlation with the conservatism of those shaping the Israeli collective memory. The Hebrew version of Wikipedia states that he was "a Jew who is considered one of the most famous false messiahs in the history of the Jewish people". The use of the word "considered" attests to the broad consensus that he was indeed a "fake" messiah.

Columnist Jacky Levy described Shabtai Zvi as a rock star whom everyone wants to forget

The English Wikipedia entry is more agnostic about his messianic claim, simply stating that he "claimed to be the long-awaited Jewish Messiah". Some scholars view Sabbateanism as the first link in a chain of Jewish movements whose ideology has centred on the expectation of redemption: from Sabbateanism to Hasidism, from Hasidism to the Zionist movement, and from there directly to the Gush Emunim movement, which, after the 1967 Six-Day War, saw the establishment of Jewish settlements in the territories captured by Israel as a sacred mission.

6. Slow decline

The small synagogue in Gaza was sold.

The failure of Nathan of Gaza's ambitious project, the deep rift it caused in the Jewish world, and his flight from Gaza represented a serious blow to the local Jewish community and to the international status of the city. Sabbateanism had become integral to the economic, religious and social lives of Jewish merchants and middlemen in Gaza, and many of them left the city when the messianic movement waned. An official census conducted in Gaza in 1690, about fifteen years after the death of Shabtai Zvi, found only twenty-six Jewish families – 100 to 150 people in all, most of the breadwinners engaged in artisanry.

The city's decline did not happen overnight and there was still some sporadic cultural activity. In 1715, one of the city's Jewish residents, Samuel Castel, produced a bilingual Hebrew-Arabic edition of the *Song of Songs*. An optimist, he worked to reinvigorate Jewish life in Gaza but was able to solicit only modest support from Egyptian Jewry. In the winter of 1753, one of the most famous Jewish sages of the time came to Gaza – Haim Joseph David Azoulai ("Hida"), whose late grandfather had served as a rabbi in the city. The grandson was esteemed not only for his erudition and books but also for his accounts of his travels, usually as an emissary to solicit funds from benefactors in Europe. He had planned to stay in Gaza for a short time en route to Egypt but had to wait fifty days before continuing his journey. This was not only because fewer convoys were passing through Gaza, but also as a result of warfare between Bedouins and peasant farmers, which made it precarious to travel to and from the city. This turmoil also adversely affected the Jews who depended on the Bedouins for their living and became another factor in the exodus of the Jewish population from Gaza. Rabbi Azoulai mentioned – apparently pleasantly surprised – that he could still find ten Jews for a minyan. In 1799, a foreign army fell upon Gaza again, this time led by Napoleon Bonaparte.

This was one of the most dramatic campaigns in the region's history, mobilising a cavalry force numbering over 20,000. The Ottomans, ostensibly reluctant to engage in battle, repeatedly employed the defensive tactic of retreat, drawing the Frenchmen into a trap. Gaza surrendered without a fight. Napoleon marched into the city at the head of his troops and did nothing to prevent the foreseeable acts of destruction, looting and violence by his soldiers following their nearly two-week trek through the desert. Many residents of Gaza fled before the French army arrived; the Jews assumed they would not be able to return to Gaza and adopted Hebron as their new permanent residence.

Napoleon aspired to capture Acre but failed. Defeated and humiliated, he retreated to Egypt without even visiting Jerusalem. He lost about 5000 men and ordered the killing of wounded French soldiers for lack of medical supplies to treat them. Napoleon's invasion did not engender any real change but left great ruin and insecurity in its wake. Gaza fell back into Ottoman hands.

In 1835, an order was issued to demolish the Great Synagogue in Gaza and its stones were used to build a fortress in Ashkelon.

It is unclear whether the synagogue was sold or expropriated, and it is possible that it was sold under duress. In any case, before handing over the synagogue the Jews were allowed to remove its carved wooden doors, adorned with a Star of David and colourful decorations; they were later installed at the Avraham Avinu Synagogue in Hebron. Their removal was a sort of symbolic, though perhaps unintentional, re-enactment of the biblical scene in which Samson rips out the gates of Gaza. Soon afterwards, as the Jewish community further dwindled, the small synagogue in Gaza was sold, with the blessing of Hebron's rabbinate.

In the late eighteenth century, Haim Farhi, a Jewish political-military adviser to the Ottoman ruler in Acre and a key architect of the city's defence against Napoleon, had tried to renew the Jewish community in Gaza. But these efforts were cut short when he was murdered in 1820 in the context of a political entanglement. It is doubtful whether any Jews still lived in Gaza at the time. Some years later, a group of former residents sent an emotional appeal to one of the wealthiest Jews in Britain, Moses Montefiore, hoping to mobilise his support for rebuilding the community in Gaza. Montefiore, who had travelled widely in the area and invested large sums to improve the lives of its Jews, is addressed in the letter as "our master, the king, who lights up the land and its dwellers with mercy". The petitioners sang the praises of Gaza, mentioning the low cost of living as one of its attributes, and asked for assistance for the indigent people who wished to return to the city "to fulfil a sacred duty at the cemetery". Montefiore did not respond to their request. In 1850, a rabbi in Jerusalem explicitly stated for the first time that there was not a single Jew in Gaza. The situation remained unchanged for another generation, and the next community to emerge in Gaza was motivated, in part, by a completely new ideology.

7. Return to Gaza

A spirit of new life would come to this city.

The belief in a return to Zion is a fundamental element of Jewish religious identity. However, some of the Jews who settled in Gaza in the 1890s primarily identified with a nascent Zionist sentiment – a national aspiration to settle the land with Jews. The waves of emigration from Europe in those years swept up many millions of people, including more than 3 million Jews. About 30,000 of them arrived in Palestine, increasing its Jewish population to about 55,000. Many of them brought Yiddish culture with them and spoke "Jewish-German". This wave of immigration, described as the First Aliyah in Zionist historiography, also included Jews from Yemen and Iraq. When the newcomers arrived, they found a small number of Jews who had already begun to establish new settlements, most of them agricultural, which served as the initial steps in a historical process that led to the founding of the State of Israel. It is hard to know how many of the immigrants were spurred by the Zionist vision; ultimately, one in every three ended up leaving. Zionism had never won the support of a majority of world Jewry. It was even subject to endless debate and scepticism among the Jews living in Palestine during the embryonic stage of Zionism. Most of them remained on the fence, finding reasons for and against the Zionist idea. One of them was the journalist Yehiel Bril.

Bril's name is not ranked high on the list of Zionist pioneers, even though he was one of the founders and a co-editor of the first Hebrew-language newspaper to be published in Palestine, *HaLevanon*. To produce the newspaper, Bril and his colleagues also established the first Hebrew printing house in Jerusalem. Bril, a native of Ukraine, arrived in Palestine in the late 1850s, when he was about twenty years old. At first, he worked as a local correspondent for *HaMagid*, a Hebrew newspaper in East Prussia, now in Poland. The Ottoman authorities shut down *HaLevanon* soon after it began publishing, and Bril published it sporadically in several European cities, including Paris, London and Mainz in Germany. He wrote extensively about Jewish immigration to Palestine and the new settlements, railing against what he saw as hasty propaganda and calling for patient and cautious planning. But as the persecution of Jews in Eastern Europe intensified, he changed his approach. In 1883, he even participated in founding one of the first settlements, Mazkeret Batya (Ekron), personally organising the arrival of a group of Jewish farmers from what is today Belarus. Bril stood out as one of the leading proponents of "Hebrew labour" – that is, replacing Arab workers with Jews. The ethos emphasised that a people that does not work its land is not worthy of it. Bril knew everyone and everyone knew him; he often lent a hand to people in need.

In 1881, he helped four families of merchants from Russia who wished to settle in Gaza. He first met them in Jaffa. They were wealthy and he was happy to assist them because it was important for him to show that it was not only destitute Jews who were coming to Palestine. The merchants planned to purchase farmland around Gaza and hire Arab labourers to work the land. This was not a simple task, not least in the legal challenges it raised, and the merchants had no idea how to proceed. One of them set off to procure millstones and a machine for grinding barley because mechanical grinders had not yet reached Gaza. But they had trouble conveying this heavy equipment to Gaza and meanwhile their money was running out. At this point, the goodhearted Bril met them and connected them with someone who agreed to offer a loan. The lender was not only intent on earning interest from the loan, but also identified with the Zionist aim of settling

This made for a total Jewish population of forty-three

Jews in Gaza and its environs. In a book he later wrote, Bril noted every detail, including the payment arrangements for the grinding machine, its mode of transport to Gaza and its operating instructions. The merchants could not proceed with their plan immediately – they first needed a permit from Constantinople.

A man named Alexander William Shapira now intervened on behalf of the merchants. He was a Russian-born Jewish convert to Christianity who worked for a British missionary society in Gaza and ran its school, which was attended by a number of Jewish pupils. Later, he also established a hospital in the city. Shapira served as a liaison between foreign citizens and the Ottoman authorities, a sort of consul general. The following months proved productive, as many Gazans brought their barley to the new mill. In time, however, the prices charged by the mill's owners began to deter customers. This made it difficult for the owners to pay back their loan and they feared their property would be confiscated. Three of them travelled to Jaffa, and Yehiel Bril was again able to find a solution. He decided to accompany them to Gaza, brimming with curiosity about the potential for developing the Zionist presence there. Travelling by carriage, they made a three-day journey from Jaffa.

About 24,000 people lived in Gaza at the time, including a few dozen Christians. The four Jewish families that Bril had assisted numbered thirty-six people. There were also three Jews from Damascus residing in the city: one was a government official and the others – a father and son – sold the fruits known as bitter apples. Another four Jews were living temporarily in Gaza: two bitter apple traders from Morocco and two metalsmiths from Jerusalem, a father-son team producing oil lamps. This made for a total Jewish population of forty-three. As he walked down Jews' Street, as it was still called, Bril noticed the remnants of *mezuzot* on many houses, a vestige of better days. The Ottoman governor of Gaza was a well-educated man, familiar with European culture, and he treated the foreigners in the city fairly. During his visit, Bril witnessed what he called an "impure incident": a Jewish woman who worked for one of the mill's owners was abducted by an Arab who had been hired to accompany her to Jerusalem; he took her to a house, where he and two of his friends abused her all night. The governor investigated, apprehended the rapists and ordered them to be flogged before they were sent to the court in Jerusalem.

When Bril's tour guide showed him a marble column and claimed it was one of the two columns that Samson ripped from the gates of the city, Bril felt duped. "That is not correct," he snapped contemptuously at his guide. "It is written in the Bible that Samson carried both columns to the top of a hill overlooking Hebron" (Book of Judges 17:3). How did the column get back to the city? Bril's reaction showed a sense of ownership: he defended his historical truth as if it were a deed to the city itself. Thousands of years after Samson chose to die with the Philistines, and long after the Philistines had passed into history, his story would provide rapturous inspiration for Israeli soldiers. Bril also saw the inscribed archaeological column that would eventually find its way to the gravesite in Rishon LeZion of the early Zionist pioneer Zvi Hirschfeld.

On one of his tours in the upper city, Bril saw a group of teenage girls leaving Shapira's mission school and making fun of their teacher, Shapira's wife. Bril made a note to himself that a Hebrew school was needed in the city. He also toured the poor neighbourhoods in the lower city, populated by peasant farmers. "Their houses are made of clay, full of vomit and manure from the animals living together with their owners in the same house," he reported. During that period, Gaza lost some of its importance as a port due to the opening of the Suez Canal a few years earlier; the ports of Beirut and Jaffa grew in prominence. Still, Bril returned from Gaza full of confidence:

There is no doubt that if there were more Europeans and Jews in this city, the ships that come and go every week between Alexandria and Beirut would also make a stop at the Gaza coast to load and unload mail and goods, and a spirit of new life would come to this city, which none of the cities in the Holy Land can rival in commerce; even Jerusalem with double the population of Gaza – cannot match it.

In the fall of 1885, settlers of Moroccan origin – about twenty families – left their homes in Jaffa and arrived in Gaza. They were persuaded to come by Kalonymos Wolf Wissotzky, founder of the tea company bearing his name and an activist in the Zionist movement in Russia.

8. The two teachers of Gaza

It is no wonder that the Jews of Gaza wholeheartedly believe in all sorts of empty nonsense.

The dreams, visions, fantasies and plans that shaped Zionist ideology were not always purely an expression of Jewish national identity; sometimes they also sprang from personal experiences. Such was the case of Zalman David Levontin, a banker born in 1856 in Belarus, then part of Russia. When he was still a schoolboy, as he later wrote, he was struck by what he read about Liberia in geography class. If the Blacks could establish a free state for themselves, there was no reason why Jews could not create a kingdom of their own in the land of their forefathers, he said to himself. Before settling in Palestine, he was in contact with proto-Zionist support groups that began to operate, primarily in Russia, under the name Hovevei Zion. These groups worked to encourage immigration to Palestine and the building of new settlements. The funding for this activity came from supporters and philanthropists like the "tea king" Kalonymus Wissotzky. Levontin was interested in the possibility of settling Jews on lands the Zionist movement would acquire from Bedouin tribes in the Gaza area: "We could live as their neighbours without any dread or fear," he wrote. "The air there is fresh and clean, and the territory is expansive. We could easily settle about 5000 families there." He also looked into the area of Rafah and El Arish, an area that likewise attracted the interest of the leader of the Zionist movement himself, Theodor Herzl.

The Bedouins received him with their traditional hospitality but it often turned out that the lands were not legally registered and it was uncertain who owned them. One time, when it seemed that everything was ready to be signed, the twelve Russian buyers slated to settle in Gaza changed their minds and decided to return home. This was not the only disappointment. "What am I doing here?" Levontin exclaimed, and he too left Palestine. Some years later, he returned as the manager of the Anglo-Palestine Bank established by the Zionist movement, in part to extend credit to settlers. In October 1913, a branch of the bank opened in Gaza, which was then home to 20,000 to 30,000 people.

Zionist historiography is sometimes inclined to boast that the first Hebrew school in Gaza was established before the Jewish bank. Previously, the small number of Jews had not warranted opening a school, so some of the residents had jointly hired a *melamed*, usually from Hebron, to provide their sons with a basic education at the level of the traditional *cheder*, while the daughters of some families had been sent to Mrs Shapira at the missionary society's school. In 1907, the renewed Jewish community numbered thirty-five to forty families, a total of about 160 people.

Four years earlier a Jewish teachers' association had been formed in Palestine, defined as a sort of "trustee" of Hovevei Zion in Odessa. One of its responsibilities was to establish Hebrew schools in the Zionist spirit, usually non-Orthodox. The primary consideration was national: the association judged that without a school in Gaza, Jews might leave the city or send their children to what was described in one of the discussions as "inciters waiting to ambush their souls" – that is, the Christian missionary society. Without a school, parents might also decide to rely on private religious instruction, an option that was regarded as equally perilous and often involved nothing more than a father teaching his son how to pray. In this context, the teachers' association, now called HaMerkaz, asked Hovevei Zion in Odessa to support the establishment of "a small school of one teacher". Starting in 1910, the association sent two teachers to Gaza, one after another. The first was Eliezer Zeldes and the second, who replaced him, was Eliyahu Yehudai, formerly Yehudov. They both came with a strong commitment to education and a profound sense of national mission, but upon their arrival in Gaza were overwhelmed with shock and a sense of alienation that persisted until they left. Most of the Jews whose children they came to teach were religious and not Ashkenazim, and they no longer lived on Jews' Street in the upper city but among Muslim Arabs, some of them wealthy. There were also some Christian Arabs in the neighbourhood.

Most of the homes were surrounded by walls and, to help allay their concerns about security, Jews felt obliged to live as close to one another as possible. Some Jews rented two homes, even leaving one of them empty, in order to distance themselves from Arab neighbours. "It was difficult for Jewish women to live among the Arabs in Gaza, who did not tolerate a woman appearing in the street without her face veiled," Zeldes wrote. Women were generally expected only to leave their homes when accompanied by a man. At night, it was also dangerous for men to go outside; the alleys were lit only by smoky lanterns. "Even though it was forbidden to keep weapons here, gunfire was frequently heard at night, and hooligans would go out to 'hunt prey' – that is, to beat up anyone who came their way," Zeldes noted. Despite the relatively high rents, the residents of the neighbourhood suffered from filth and neglect, as did the rest of the city. Most of the homes lacked efficient sewerage systems, which made it particularly unpleasant in summer: "Together with the heat, Gaza became one big latrine," Zeldes reported.

"The cultural situation in Gaza is very deficient ... there are no books"

He published his observations in a new Hebrew socio-democratic newspaper, *Hapoel Hatzair*, and he clearly tried to temper his criticism. Before describing the stench that pervaded the city's alleyways, he noted that "Gaza is beautiful from afar" and, like many others, praised its pleasant climate and the splendour of the fields around it. Similarly, what he had to say about the children's parents came only after stating that "the Jews in Gaza are far superior to their Arab neighbours". But he finally shared his frank assessment: "The cultural situation in Gaza is very deficient and other than a prayer book, a book of psalms and such, there are no books. Therefore, it is no wonder that the Jews of Gaza wholeheartedly believe in all sorts of empty nonsense ... the evil eye, ghosts and demons." In letters he published in the newspaper, Zeldes commended the pupils and their parents for their diligence and great joy in learning, and he basked in the love they showered upon him. But after two years, he could no longer withstand the difficulties, and he left.

His replacement, Yehudai, wrote only to his superiors and not for publication, and he did not mince his words: He complained that he was suffering "the torments of hell". As a native of Bulgaria, he noted that he too was Sephardi, like most of the local Jews. Nonetheless, he struggled to find his place among the "primitive" Jews of Gaza, as he described them. His writings indicate that two of his pupils' parents sold supplies to three new Jewish settlements built near Gaza and five parents conducted commerce with the Bedouins; three were moneylenders, two were tailors and two were metalsmiths.

A visit to the home of one of the families engendered an anthropological description, as if Yehudai had returned from an exotic land: "Four thick walls are topped by a dome in the form of two intersecting arches. There are no windows, only in the dome – one or two round windows that faintly light the upper part of the room. The middle is immersed in dancing shadows and below are varying depths of darkness: dimness into which the eyes of a person coming from outside cannot immediately penetrate upon entering." The interior design was, in his words, "part Robinson Crusoe, part European", with a large mirror in a gilded frame "entirely carved with garlands and flowers", white lace curtains adorned with red silk ribbons, and a white sofa "which, though there was a sheet spread over it, had lumps of knotted rags and worn-out tatters protruding from beneath it, as if in defiance". Hanging on one of the walls was a Martini-Henry rifle. "If I hadn't seen you at the synagogue, I would never have believed that you are Jews," he concluded. One of the long-time members of the community recalled the days when many of the Arab men in Gaza carried pistols and draped themselves with bandoliers.

The immediate problem was that the children were not fluent in Hebrew; most of them spoke Arabic with their parents. "With their Arabic jargon mixed with strange Hebrew words, it is impossible to recognise them among their Muslim or Christian neighbours," Yehudai wrote. They walked around barefoot wearing a type of robe and had dirty fingernails. He was particularly repulsed when they kissed his hands. His pupils – about twenty boys and girls of various ages – were divided into two age groups and spent up to seven hours a day at school, mainly focusing on reading and writing Hebrew, arithmetic and English. They studied the Book of Judges in Bible lessons and the Great Wall of China in geography. On the rare occasions when the teacher obtained a textbook, he would tear out the pages and distribute them among the children. There were also art lessons and exercise classes. Prayer lessons were assigned to a special *melamed*.

The letters of Yehudai from Gaza, preserved in the Archive of Jewish Education at Tel Aviv University, were written as an expression of personal distress, yet also reflected the nearly impervious barriers to developing a shared set of basic values for the new Jewish society in Palestine. The parents, especially those of Moroccan origin, evidently felt a similar sense of alienation towards their children's teacher. From the very first day, they argued with him about almost everything, from technical and monetary matters to the curriculum. Some parents were opposed to having boys and girls learn together, and some demanded more religious studies, or that the children learn French instead of English. There was also the question of corporal punishment as a disciplinary measure. "Yes, I am also against corporal punishment, but theory is one thing and practice is another," wrote Yehudai. So he occasionally hit unruly children on the wrist with a ruler. Some parents threatened to transfer their children to the missionary society's school. "The missionary society is their most powerful weapon," Yehudai wrote in reference to some parents. "They believe in the Messiah and reject the need for education in general." A rabbi named Nissim Ohana, a native of Algeria who settled in Gaza and later relocated to New York, co-authored a book entitled *Know What to Answer* with the mufti of Gaza in an effort to counter missionary activity.

Mordechai Elkayam, who had attended the school, confirmed in his memoirs that the two teachers failed to integrate into the community and he attributed this to narrow-mindedness and cultural arrogance. Most members of the community had grown up in an Arab milieu, primarily in North Africa, and the two teachers refused to understand why they clung to their native lifestyle. Elkayam complained that Zeldes "expected them to be what Jews were in Europe" and had "exaggerated expectations" about the level of cleanliness in an Arab city. Zeldes refused to accept that the pupils' parents sat in cafés and smoked water pipes. Again and again, he warned parents not to allow their children to go barefoot so that they would not catch a cold or contract tuberculosis. But the parents would respond that they were not in Russia. Some parents agitated for replacing Zeldes with a teacher who would not look condescendingly upon the community, but most of them simply ignored what he said. Elkayam did admit that "some of the parents were of a low level" and did not recognise their children's need for schooling. "How much longer will I suffer from these predators?" exclaimed

The Jewish children would decorate the sukkah with colourful paper chains, eat sweets and sing holiday songs

Yehudai. The absence of his wife, who did not accompany him to far-off Gaza, had "drained" him, he wrote. He also had to remind his superiors repeatedly that they were late in paying his wages.

When Yehudai's pupil Mordechai Elkayam grew up and became a father himself, he looked back nostalgically on his childhood. His memories evoke a warm and inspiring atmosphere of family and community. He recalled how the Jewish children in the neighbourhood would decorate the sukkah with colourful paper chains, eat sweets and sing holiday songs. During Passover, everyone at the Seder table would wear a long white tunic and carry a white sack on their back to re-enact the exodus from Egypt. The matzot they ate were baked in a joint effort with neighbours and friends from the community. Each person was assigned a particular role – one was responsible for flour and another brought water, while a third was in charge of the baking. All this took place amid singing and merry-making. Elkayam also recalled how his uncle tried to convince his father to leave Gaza and join his business in Jaffa, and how his father responded: "I'm not budging from Gaza." This conversation would replay year after year, as if the script were part of the holiday prayers.

Nearly every child in Gaza, Elkayam recounted, whether Jew or Arab, adorned himself with a small dagger inlaid with beads. On Sundays, some Jewish teenagers would ride their parents' horses, which were bedecked with chains and decorated with colourful wool sacks on their chests, galloping triumphantly to a picnic in the garden of a Christian home. Elkayam's father, Nissim, had been involved in establishing the school in consultation with Eliezer Ben-Yehuda, a central figure in reviving the Hebrew language, who took an interest in the Jewish community of Gaza. In fact, Ben-Yehuda had proposed the school's name: Samson. It seems, however, that the school was not the community's top interest. The local bank, on the other hand, elicited their fascination.

The bank manager Abraham Elmalih, whose family came from Morocco, had worked as a teacher in Damascus before relocating to Gaza to run the bank. The first bank in the city, it remained the only one for a long time. It was mainly involved in extending credit to its customers, predominantly Arabs. "Our objective in establishing the bank in Gaza," Elmalih later wrote, "was not only to lend material assistance and moral support to the small Hebrew community and to all of [Gaza's] residents, irrespective of religion, but also and primarily to increase the Jewish population and create a centre of settlement that could provide a livelihood for thousands of Hebrew families."

Elmalih was considered the No. 1 Jew in the city, well connected with the authorities, including the police. He would sometimes demonstrate his high standing by riding a horse while arrayed in a magnificent cloak. One time, when a Jew came to ask for his help after an Arab had stolen three of his donkeys. Elmalih summoned the police commander and, in light of the bank manager's status, an extensive manhunt was launched. The thief had fled to a certain village, and the local mukhtar refused to turn him in. The police commander ordered the mukhtar's arrest until he agreed to cooperate. Elmalih, who obviously knew something about Ottoman methods of interrogation, felt pangs of conscience and reminded the police commander that it was illegal to employ such methods. The commander replied: "Do you want the law or the donkeys?" The next day, the mukhtar broke down and the donkeys were returned to their owner.

A number of new settlements established not far from Gaza – including Gedera (1884), Be'er Tuvia (1888) and Ruhama (1911) – functioned as satellite communities and bolstered the Jewish community in the city. Meanwhile, in the annals of the Ottoman Empire it was a period of decline: the Young Turk Revolution and the Balkan Wars marked the beginning of the end. Like empires that had preceded it, the Ottoman Empire concluded its centuries of rule in the region with a regime of tyranny, corruption and decay. It is somewhat puzzling, then, that the Ottomans worked on plans to build a large and modern residential neighbourhood on the strip of sand stretching between Gaza and the sea. The Rimal ("Sands") project was intended in part to enhance the city's defence, but it also attracted the interest of such leaders of Zionist settlement as Zalman David Levontin, who decided to build a residential project for Jews on the outskirts of Gaza. The model for this was Ahuzat Bayit – the project built on the outskirts of Arab Jaffa that eventually became Tel Aviv. In both cases, the developers followed the fundamental Zionist principle of not settling Jews inside Arab cities, only alongside them.

Nissim Elkayam exerted great efforts to integrate Gaza into the Zionist enterprise and spoke about "tens of thousands" of future residents. But the Zionist settlement planners had second thoughts about the Gaza project. Among other reasons, they concluded that it would mainly attract religious and non-Ashkenazi Jews of low income. Jews from Russia would not want to settle there. The researcher Zvi Shiloni saw this as a missed opportunity of historic proportions. But he also noted the primary reason why the plan was never implemented: Gaza was again destroyed by foreign conquerors – this time the soldiers of the British Empire.

9. Massacre and flight

It was a first sign that the end was approaching.

World War I created a situation in which most of the Jews in Palestine, being of Russian origin, were suddenly classified as enemy citizens. When thousands were presented with the choice of enlisting in the

Ottoman army or leaving the country, most opted for the latter and relocated to Egypt. The Jews in Gaza who did not leave of their own volition were forced to do so in two waves: initially they were expelled along with other foreign citizens and subsequently as part of the entire Gazan population. British forces under General Edmund Allenby finally conquered the city in November 1917, having twice been repelled by the Ottomans. Among the more than 3000 British soldiers killed in this conflict and buried in a military cemetery not far from Gaza were Jews, whose gravestones are marked with the Star of David. Meanwhile, the British government decided to support the aspirations of the Zionist movement, and Foreign Secretary Arthur James Balfour issued a historic declaration expressing support for establishing a "national home" for the Jewish people in Palestine.

The fierce battles waged by the British to conquer Palestine caused widespread damage. Its repair became one of the first tasks facing the British military government, prior to the establishment of the civil Mandatory regime in 1920. Gaza was clearly not a top priority. Meanwhile, in the autumn of 1919, one Jewish family took the initiative of making its home in Gaza, at least for a while. Tzila and Lazar Margolin had arrived in Palestine in 1906 as refugees from a pogrom in Odessa. The couple and their three children lived in various places, finding it hard to decide where to settle. The owner of a flour mill in Gedera suggested they take over an abandoned mill in Gaza, and they followed his advice. It was not an ideological decision; in fact, Tzila was opposed to the idea. "There was still great desolation in the city," she later told her granddaughter, the Israeli writer Yehudit Katzir. Everywhere you looked there were broken walls with piles of rubble alongside them. In time, more Jews came to live there, including members of the community who had been expelled to Cairo when World War I broke out and were no longer young. Most of the Jews in the renewed community had come from Europe and had not grown up immersed in Arab culture. Some were government officials, while others, including two physicians and a pharmacist, worked in professions that were of use to the Arab population. From 1924, an airport operated in Gaza, serving as a stopover on the India–Egypt route, and soon afterwards, a small hotel was opened in the city by a Jewish woman, Hanna Yoffe. The Jews in Gaza, nearly 100 people, were a random mix rather than a homogeneous community and often quarrelled with each other. The school, which had Arabs among its pupils, was in poor shape and some members of the community despised the new teacher.

From the 1920s, the Jewish community in Gaza also had to contend with the emergence of Palestinian Arab nationalism. However, personal relations between local Jews and Arabs did not always reflect the intensity of the violent national conflict that began to unfold in Palestine. Tzila Margolin's daughter, for example, recalled having Arab girlfriends in Gaza and said she never encountered hostility from her Arab neighbours. Similarly, Eliezer Zeldes wrote: "The relations between Arabs and Jews are very good and a Jew has never suffered for being a Jew." This was, at best, only part of the picture. Mordechai Elkayam recalled a brawl between Arab and Jewish teenagers in Gaza. Following this incident, it was decided that the Jewish teens would finish their school day an hour before or after the Arabs. As Elkayam noted, this was a first sign that the end was approaching.

Incidents between Jews and Arabs in other cities often had an impact on life in Gaza. In 1921, clashes between Jews and Arabs in Jerusalem prompted most of Gaza's Jews to leave the city. There were later efforts to persuade them to return, but their future was not guaranteed. "This small community is not yet permanent," Yitzhak Ben-Zvi wrote to his wife after visiting Gaza in 1921. "Its future is uncertain. Only with a larger settlement will it be possible to ensure our future in this important spot." The Jews persevered in Gaza until the massacre in Hebron on Saturday, 24 August 1929, when about seventy members of the Jewish community were murdered. The immediate trigger was a dispute between Jews and Arabs regarding prayers at the Western Wall in Jerusalem; the proximity of Tisha B'Av and the Prophet Mohammed's birthday further fuelled the tension.

Incidents between Jews and Arabs in other cities often had an impact on life in Gaza

In Gaza, the troubles already had begun on the Thursday afternoon, according to Eliezer Margolin. A Jewish police sergeant instructed the local Jews to gather at Hanna Yoffe's hotel, and they complied. The next day, after Friday prayers at the Great Mosque, dozens of Arab men assembled across from the hotel, some of them carrying clubs, daggers and swords. Policemen tried unsuccessfully to disperse them. The hotel's owner demanded safe passage for the Jews to the police station. Later, she collected some sharp knives from the kitchen and her son fetched hatchets and iron bars from the storage room. The women and children went up to the second floor. The Arabs chanted "Death to the Jews!" Yoffe demanded that the policemen – some of whom were Arabs – use their guns, but they said their orders were to hold their fire. No one slept that night and in the morning the crowd outside the hotel swelled. Yoffe again urged the policemen to open fire, and a single shot was discharged, but it was too late and a number of Arabs broke into the building. One of them attacked a Jew with a dagger, but the target of the assault was the pharmacist, who retaliated by spraying his assailant with acid. The man fled, screaming in pain, and the other Arabs followed. Later, English police officers arrived and opened fire. When the area in front of the hotel was finally cleared, the Jews were transferred to the police station in three cars as Arabs hurled rocks at them. The mayor, Sa'id al-Shawwa, arrived at the police station with his three sons, who tried to calm the mob and stop the torrent of rocks. One of the mayor's sons was struck by a rock. With great effort, they managed to squeeze the besieged Jews into cars and drive them to the train station, advising them to lie on the floor of the train cars as the barrage of rocks continued. One of the mayor's sons rode with the Jews to Tel Aviv.

The rioting spread from Hebron to Safed and other locations, and dozens of Jews and Arabs were killed. The British police later helped a few Jews to return to Gaza, settle their business affairs and collect the rest of their belongings, most of which they found untouched, though some had been burned or looted. The Jews felt that they were drawing the curtain on many generations of history in Gaza. In the following years, only a small number of Jews visited the city. Among them was a group of schoolchildren on their annual field trip. "I remember the trip to Gaza," wrote one of the schoolboys, Yitzhak Rabin, who later became prime minister of Israel. "We slept in a school, in the centre of the city. Arab children congregated outside. We stayed inside, our hearts gripped with fear."

10. Iron walls

David Ben-Gurion had no need for Samson mythology.

A few months after the expulsion of 1929, the Rosh Hashanah edition of the *Doar HaYom* newspaper featured an excerpt, translated into Hebrew, from a new Russian novel – *Samson the Nazarite* by Ze'ev Jabotinsky. A journalist and statesman, Jabotinsky led the right-wing Revisionist opposition in the Zionist movement. Of course, Jabotinsky was not the first person to draw inspiration from the story of Samson. His predecessors included some of the greatest artists, musicians and writers in history – Rembrandt, Rubens, Handel, Milton and many more. The mythological hero also provided inspiration for Israeli poets and writers such as David Grossman, as well as authors of children's literature. The American film director Cecil B. DeMille drew on Jabotinsky's book when he produced and directed his Oscar-winning film *Samson and Delilah*. Jabotinsky's *Samson*, however, was not a matter of romance or entertainment; rather, it defined a national objective.

The chapter Jabotinsky chose to present to the newspaper's readers, so soon after the Jewish presence in Gaza had been erased, was entitled "Samson's Testament". One of the hero's men, Hermesh, informs Samson about a violent Philistine campaign conducted among the Jews in Tyre to collect taxes and search for weapons – referred to in the story as "iron". As the Philistines went from house to house, none of the Jews attempted to defend themselves – except for one of the city elders, Abiram. A dignified and proud man, he stood at the entrance to his home and shouted "No!" The Philistine commander ordered him to be flogged on the spot, in the middle of the street. No one stood up to defend him. Samson asks Hermesh when this occurred, and on hearing the answer, he clenches his fist. It had happened a week before he attended a banquet with the Philistine commander, who embraced him, sang songs and said nothing about the recent operation in Tyre. Samson suddenly realises that the Philistines often abuse the Jews like this, behind his back, and then invite him to a banquet where he entertains them with riddles and parables as if nothing had happened. How had he failed to see this? It is now so clear to him.

Samson is sitting with Hermesh at the seashore. Then he gets up, places his hand on his guest's shoulder and paces back and forth without saying a word. Hermesh, concerned, asks if all is well with him. "I live a life of joy and in the future the joy will be even greater!" Samson responds. Confused, Hermesh says that he must take his leave and asks Samson what he should say to his friends. Samson ponders for a moment and says that only two words should be conveyed in his name. The first is "iron" – that is, weapons. "They should collect iron and pay for it with whatever they have: money, wheat, oil, wine, their flocks and even their wives and daughters: everything for iron. Nothing in the world is as valuable as iron." Hermesh promises to convey his message, saying that his friends will understand it. As for the second word, explains Samson, they might not understand it right away, but it is also vital – "King!" "One man will give the sign and thousands of people will raise their arm as one. This is the custom of the Philistines and that is why the Philistines are the masters of the Land of Canaan. Spread my word from Tyre to Hebron and from Shechem and onwards – 'King!'" Hermesh promises to do this and kisses Samson's hand.

The Philistines in this scene represent the Arabs and Samson represents Jabotinsky himself. The message is that the Jews must no longer live as a minority in an Arab land lest they suffer a similar fate to the Jews of Gaza. Rather, the Jews must live as a solid majority in an independent state surrounded by an "iron wall". The military might of the Jewish state will convince the Arabs that it cannot be destroyed. When the Arabs realise

One of the first units of the IDF deployed in the Gaza area in 1948 was called "Samson's Foxes"

this and stop opposing the state's existence, they can be accepted as citizens with equal rights. The idea had crystallised in Jabotinsky's mind several years before writing his Samson novel and had won considerable support. One of the first units of the Israel Defense Forces deployed in the Gaza area in 1948 was called "Samson's Foxes". By then, Jabotinsky was no longer alive.

David Ben-Gurion had no need for Samson mythology. Long before Jabotinsky expressed his idea of an "iron wall", Ben-Gurion was guided by the principle that Zionism's success depended on the ability of Jews to defend themselves against the Arabs and to prove the futility of any attempts to destroy them. In 1906, three years after arriving from Poland as a young man of twenty, Ben-Gurion worked as a labourer on a farm in the Galilee; he also believed in "Hebrew labour". Arabs attacked the farm with gunfire and one of the labourers was killed before his eyes. It was a formative experience that led Ben-Gurion to study the possibilities for living with the Arabs. For a while, he hoped to find the answer in the reading room of the New York Public Library, where he conducted research for a book on the history of the Land of Israel, co-authored with Yitzhak Ben-Zvi and published in 1918. The two reached the conclusion that a large percentage of the Arabs in Palestine were descendants of Jews from biblical times who had been forced to convert during the Islamic conquest. If everyone is a Jew, this solves the problem, the two believed. Their best-selling book included a chapter documenting the decline of Gaza during World War I. However, in view of its illustrious past, the two authors promised a "bright future" for the city.

The idyllic atmosphere of the public library in Manhattan quickly faded into the past when Ben-Gurion returned to Palestine with the occupying British army. In a discussion on the future of Jews and Arabs conducted in Jaffa in 1919, he sounded more realistic: "Everyone sees the difficulty of relations between Jews and Arabs," he began, "but not everyone sees that there is no solution to that question. There is no solution. There is an abyss, and nothing can fill that abyss." Two nations were facing off against each other, he continued: "We want Palestine to be ours as a nation – the Arabs want it to be theirs as a nation ... I don't know what Arab would agree to Palestine belonging to the Jews."

This was the foundational perspective that shaped Ben-Gurion's approach to statecraft and security for the rest of his life. From one war to the next, an increasing number of Israelis adopted this outlook too: there are two national identities, both grounded in a sense of attachment to the entire homeland. Any territorial compromise chips away at the internal integrity of each of the two identities and is thus possible as a temporary arrangement at most. In other words, given the impossibility of resolving the conflict, the imperative is to manage it. This formulation became the consensus view over time, from war to war. Despite that, profound and emotionally charged disagreements not only divided the two antagonists but also deepened the internal rifts on both sides, ultimately fuelling the catastrophe of 2023.

11. War and statehood

War does not operate according to the Bible.

During its thirty-year rule in Palestine, Britain supported the Zionist movement and generally helped it achieve Ben-Gurion's goal: an independent state with the largest possible Jewish majority, covering the broadest possible territory, with the fewest possible Arab inhabitants. The British allowed the Zionist movement to build hundreds of new communities, including several cities, to populate them with hundreds of thousands of Jewish immigrants, and to develop the economic, political, social, military and cultural underpinnings of the longed-for state. There was resistance from the Arabs.

With the rise of the Nazis in Germany, the demographics shifted as tens of thousands of Jewish refugees arrived. The Arabs responded with a series of violent actions known as the Arab Revolt. The British decided that Palestine was no longer worth the price it demanded of them and in 1937 proposed dividing it into two states. It was not an original proposal: in the three decades that preceded it, at least ten other plans had been proposed for dividing the land between the Jews and Arabs. None of them apportioned Gaza to the Jews.

Ben-Gurion was not enthusiastic when he first read the British proposal – the Peel Plan, named for Lord William Peel, who chaired the royal commission that drafted it. But he took another look at the plan that evening and noted that the British were advocating the compulsory transfer of Arabs living in the territories earmarked for the Jewish state. He made a note of this in his diary and underlined the words "compulsory transfer". He told his colleagues: "I saw two positive things in the Peel Plan – the idea of a state and compulsory transfer". He did not view the latter as something immoral, he emphasised. The idea had accompanied the Zionist movement since its earliest days, appearing in Theodor Herzl's diary.

Starting in the 1930s, the Zionist movement engaged in preparing for the "voluntary transfer" of Arabs. The idea was not to rely on the free decision of each individual Arab, but rather to pursue an international agreement that would allow the transfer of an entire population, regardless of their wishes. A committee was formed to advance the idea of transfer. Its discussions were practical and focused: who would be evacuated first, farmers or city dwellers (the committee preferred to transfer farmers first); how long it would take to execute the transfer (they envisioned a ten-year period); and where the Arabs would be sent (as far away as possible, anywhere from Gaza to Baghdad). The numbers changed from one meeting to the next, but some spoke of evacuating up to 100,000 Arab families. Only a few Zionist leaders opposed the transfer plans in principle, some of them objecting on moral grounds or contending that a population transfer of sufficient scope could only be implemented in wartime. The perception was that Zionism could only take root in territory that was empty – or nearly empty – of Arabs.

The murder of 6 million Jews who could have settled in Palestine and played a role in creating a liberal European society had inflicted a serious blow to the Zionist dream. Zionists regarded the Holocaust as affirming the prognosis that had engendered the movement to establish a Jewish state, and they stepped up their diplomatic, set-

The feeling among the Zionist leadership was that it was now or never

tlement and military activity accordingly. At least two other partition maps were subsequently proposed. One was drawn by Ben-Gurion and the second was sketched during negotiations that culminated in the formal United Nations partition resolution in 1947. Both maps left Gaza for the Arabs. There were different nuances, and plenty of politics, but the feeling among the Zionist leadership was that it was now or never. Prior to the anticipated UN discussion on partition, eleven embryonic settlements were established one night in October 1946, with the aim of creating "facts on the ground" to ensure that the territory would remain in the Jewish state. One of these eleven settlements was built on the outskirts of Gaza.

The day after the partition decision – approved by the UN General Assembly on 29 November 1947 – the national conflict erupted in full force, initially within the bounds of what is still described as "civil war". During the months that preceded Israel's declaration of independence in May 1948, hundreds of thousands of Arabs became refugees, many of them fleeing to the neighbouring Arab countries that immediately invaded Israel after it declared its independence. The war lasted some twenty months and nearly 6000 Israelis were killed, about 1 per cent of its population at the time. It ended in a series of armistice agreements, one of which left Gaza under Egyptian rule.

Even before the guns fell silent, a historical, political and moral dispute arose that has never been resolved: the Arabs claimed that the Israelis had forcibly expelled them. In response, the Israelis accused the Arabs of starting the war, also contending that the refugees were acting, in part, in response to their leaders' promise of a return to their homes after the destruction of Israel. Over the years, the historical research has come to rely less upon the personal memories of refugees and more on Israeli archives, including classified military operational reports. It has become clear that not everything that happened in one place occurred in other places at the same time, in the same way and on the same scale. One thing is undisputed: the government of Israel refused to allow the refugees, some 700,000 people, to return. For the Arabs of Palestine, this became the Nakba, their national tragedy. Nearly 200,000 of them were exiled to Gaza, tripling its population, and nowhere else did the Arab–Israeli conflict become more severe. During the war, Ben-Gurion put the brakes on an operation designed to conquer Gaza, in part due to pressure from Britain and the United States. In view of the hundreds of thousands of refugees in Gaza, it made no sense to capture it. At one cabinet meeting during the war, Ben-Gurion voiced his thoughts on Gaza: "It would be good if we could eject the Egyptians from Gaza as well," he said. "But we won't seize Gaza, for it is doubtful whether Gaza should be within the bounds of our country and it is very doubtful whether anyone would allow us to make Gaza part of the country." He added parenthetically, "According to the Bible, we also deserve Sinai, but war does not operate according to the Bible."

Similarly, Ben-Gurion refrained from capturing the West Bank and even East Jerusalem. This was all consistent with a principle that had guided the Zionist movement from the start: a small territory without Arabs is preferable to a large territory with an Arab-majority population. Ben-Gurion's political rivals, primarily from the nationalist right, frequently accused him of defeatism. In the early 1950s, direct and indirect negotiations on amendments to the armistice accord with Egypt led to a proposal to cede the entire Gaza Strip – with all its inhabitants – to Israel. Ben-Gurion debated whether the expansion of Israel's borders to include the Gaza coastline, pushing the Egyptians into the desert in the process, justified the absorption of hundreds of thousands of Arabs beyond the 100,000 or so already living in Israel. In the end, the cabinet opted for Ben-Gurion's recommendation that, "if it becomes possible," Israel would agree to take what is today called the Gaza Strip with all its residents. "We will need to treat the Arabs as if they were Jews," he said. The notes in his war diary and his comments from the cabinet meeting reflect an ambivalent attitude: an aversion to absorbing Gaza versus a belief that it was necessary and possible to capture it, or even "do away" with it – as he wrote in one diary entry.

The refugee problem weighed heavily on Ben-Gurion's mind. His diary reflects a constant need to convince himself that the Arabs were to blame for their own tragedy, that there was no alternative but to expel them, and that most of the refugees would be absorbed into Arab countries and in time forget their past and their homeland. Coming from a leader of a people that for 2000 years had kept alive a dream of returning from exile, it was a curious assessment. And indeed, the Palestinian refugees did not forget their homeland. In fact, the refugee problem only grew worse. As the living conditions in the camps deteriorated and their population increased, they cultivated their collective identity as exiles and refugees, and instilled it from one generation to the next. Egypt, which assumed control of the Gaza Strip, encouraged Palestinian refugees to join the *fedayeen*, a group whose name means "those who sacrifice themselves". The fedayeen attacked both Israeli civilians and military targets. In contrast to the West Bank, and particularly East Jerusalem, Gaza stirred almost no national-religious longings among Israelis. Most saw it only as a curse that no one knew how to remove. Israeli slang coined the expression "Go to Gaza" as a way to say "Go to hell" – a play on words in Hebrew.

12. The glint of the blade

The gates of Gaza were too heavy for his shoulders.

Ben-Gurion stepped down as prime minister in late 1953, but returned to the government in early 1955 as defence minister. Soon afterwards, the IDF launched an operation in the Gaza Strip in retaliation for a fedayeen attack in which the infiltrators stole sensitive top-secret documents. The IDF operation, dubbed Operation Black Arrow, was the largest reprisal attack in Gaza since Israel's formation and culminated in the death of some thirty-seven Arabs and eight Israelis.

Fedayeen activity intensified. A particularly brutal attack on a wedding celebration at a communal settlement, Moshav Patish, in March 1955 seems to have impaired Ben-Gurion's judgement. He summoned the IDF chief of staff, Moshe Dayan, and asked him three questions: Could Israel seize the Gaza Strip quickly? Is the IDF prepared for a war against Egypt? Is the IDF prepared for a war against all of the Arab states? A few days later, after informing the cabinet that Dayan had replied affirmatively to all his questions, he proposed "expelling the Egyptians" from the Gaza Strip. He assumed that the Palestinian refugees in Gaza would also be removed, though it was not clear how he imagined this happening. The minutes from the meeting reflect emotional tumult. The Gaza Strip must be conquered to ensure "the existence of the Jewish people", Ben-Gurion argued. To dispel any doubts, he reiterated that "this is not a question of the state. It is a question of the Jewish people." He assumed that the IDF could expel the Egyptian army from the Strip, but asked himself what to do with the refugees. "I assume that some will flee to Hebron. These borders are porous. I know them – they'll flee there," he said. At the time, Hebron was under Jordan's jurisdiction and Ben-Gurion did not dismiss the possibility that the Jordanians would try to prevent the entry of refugees and perhaps even open fire on them. "If they fire at them – so be it," he decided. Yes, there would be an outcry in the world: "There was also a great outcry about 800,000 refugees! ... we withstood that ... in any case, if they cry out – so be it. Later, they'll get used to it."

Some government ministers had heard such outbursts from Ben-Gurion in the past; Gaza was not the only obsession that provoked him from time to time. But most of the ministers were horrified. Ben-Gurion tried to persuade them: "You have children and I have children. You must safeguard their future. I don't want your grandchildren and my grandchildren to be annihilated." This was a clear allusion to the Holocaust. "We have to protect the children before it is too late," he said. He assured the ministers that he did not see the proposed operation as a solution for reconstituting the historical territories and borders. It was only an operation to expel the enemy. When he realised that opposition among the ministers remained strong, he proposed an alternative: seizing the northern part of the Strip and pushing its residents southwards. One of the ministers politely suggested that Ben-Gurion give them a night to think it over. The proposal was put to a vote the next day and rejected by a large majority.

On 29 April 1956, preparations were underway for the joint wedding of four couples at Kibbutz Nahal Oz, which had been established several hundred metres from the border with the Gaza Strip in 1951. The guest of honour was the IDF chief of staff, Dayan. When he arrived, he learnt that the local commander, Roi Rotberg, had set out on horseback to drive off several Palestinian farmers who had crossed the border to pasture their flocks and plunder the kibbutz's fields. When he arrived at the site, Rotberg was shot and killed. His murderers later returned his mutilated body to UN observers. Dayan's eulogy over his grave turned Rotberg into an Israeli icon. (Dayan, a skilled writer, sometimes also wrote poetry.) Like others before him, Dayan described the war with the Palestinians as an inescapable decree of fate: "A generation of settlement are we, and without the steel helmet and the cannon's maw we will not be able to plant a tree and build a house."

This was not a new idea, nor was there anything original in stating that "the millions of Jews who were annihilated without a land are watching us from the ashes of Israeli history and command us to settle and rebuild a land for our people". The novel element in Dayan's address was an expression of understanding for the Palestinians' animosity: "For eight years they have been sitting in refugee camps in Gaza and before their eyes we are turning the soil and villages where they and their ancestors dwelled into our inheritance." Therefore, "it was only natural that a sea of hatred and longings for revenge are swelling within them". Rotberg, who had been a peace-seeking young man, failed to see this, said Dayan, thus implying that Rotberg and his like-minded friends were partly to blame for his death: "The light in his heart blinded his eyes and he did not see the glint of the blade. The longing for peace deafened his ears and he did not hear the voice of the murderers waiting in ambush." These words correspond with the feelings of Samson in Jabotinsky's novel when Hermesh tells him how the Philistines are deceiving him. Dayan, too, thought of the biblical hero. He described Rotberg as an innocent blond youth who lacked sufficient physical strength: "The gates of Gaza were too heavy for his shoulders and vanquished him."

It was in October 1956, on the eve of capturing the Gaza Strip and Sinai Peninsula in collaboration with France and Britain, that Ben-Gurion made the statement about Gaza quoted earlier: "If I believed in miracles, I'd wish for it to be swallowed up by the sea." The shared objective of what became known as the Suez Campaign was to topple the Egyptian president, Abdel Nasser. This was the "second round". The idea was for Israel to attack Egypt, prompting it to return fire; then Britain and France would call upon both sides to end hostilities. Israel would agree to a ceasefire and Egypt would refuse, and British and French forces would join the Israeli attack. The overthrow of Nasser was designed to abort the nationalisation of the Suez Canal and ensure Israel's freedom of navigation in the Gulf of Eilat. Part of the incentive that led Ben-Gurion to collaborate with France came to light years later: the French had promised assistance in developing Israel's nuclear potential.

The "second round", in which the IDF captured the Sinai Peninsula and Gaza from Egypt, stirred great patriotic pride in Israelis. During the previous eight years, more than 1000 Israelis had been victims of Arab terror operations. Ben-Gurion wrote that

Tiran Island, located at the entrance to the Gulf of Eilat, would again be part of the "Third Kingdom of Israel". This was unfortunate wording and he quickly retracted his statement, but they reflected an emotional response that suddenly included the occupation of Gaza. Major Mordechai Elkayam, whose grandfather had been the Jewish community's leader in Gaza half a century earlier, was appointed deputy military governor. Elkayam later recounted that while serving in this role, he rescued one of the mayor's sons from a terrorist who was about to kill him, thus reciprocating the mayor's help in saving the Jews in 1929. The need to show historical continuity was also expressed in the campaign's official name – Operation Kadesh. The Bible says that Moses dispatched the spies from Kadesh to reconnoitre the Land of Canaan during the Exodus. One of Israel's first actions in Gaza was to erase the vestiges of Egyptian rule, such as monuments memorialising fallen fedayeen.

The need to show historical continuity was expressed in the campaign's official name – Operation Kadesh

The military administration in Gaza adopted procedures from the military government that placed restrictions on about 100,000 Israeli Arabs. Most of them were in the Galilee, and among them were refugees who had infiltrated back across the border. During Israel's four-month occupation of the Gaza Strip, it began to take over the education, health and transportation systems, as well as the local population registry. Everything was done on the assumption that Gaza would remain Israeli forever, as Prime Minister

Ben-Gurion declared a number of times – even though he never really wanted this and knew it would not happen. The United States and the Soviet Union demanded that Israel withdraw from the Gaza Strip and Sinai Peninsula, and Israel complied, pulling out its forces in March 1957. Gaza returned to Egyptian control and a UN force was also deployed there. Israel received guarantees of freedom of navigation in the Gulf of Eilat. Most Israelis felt that their country was being treated unjustly, as in the "first round", when the borders of the new state were demarcated and Gaza and the West Bank, including East Jerusalem, were left outside them. The withdrawal from Sinai and Gaza thus laid the ideological, emotional and political foundations that would guide Israel following its victory in the "third round".

13. Six-Day War

*The murder shook Israel and marked the end of the
"enlightened occupation".*

In the first half of the 1960s, Israel came to be seen as a success story in nearly every field, except for the constant threat from its neighbours to its very existence. The border with Egypt was relatively quiet, but the danger from Palestinian organisations heightened during the second half of the decade. The most prominent of these was Fatah, established several years earlier and led by Yasser Arafat. Most of the Palestinian infiltrations to Israel came via Jordan and Syria, and these actions entangled the entire Middle East. Israel responded with reprisal operations in Jordan and downed several Syrian MiG aircraft. With Egypt tied to Syria in a defence pact, another war was a reasonable likelihood.

And then, to the complete surprise of many, the fragility of Israeli society became apparent. Just four out of every ten Jews living in Israel in 1967 were native-born, while the other six came from nearly every corner of the earth. There were over a million recent immigrants, mainly from Eastern Europe, many of them Holocaust survivors. Nearly half a million Israelis, about a fifth of the population, had lived in Israel for less than a decade and were not fluent in Hebrew. Most had not come to Israel by choice, but as refugees with nowhere else to go, many from Muslim countries and many of low socio-economic standing.

As long as it seemed that the state was building a stable and healthy society, integrating into the Western world and promising its citizens both national and personal growth, they could still believe in the Israeli dream. But by 1967, the country had sunk into an economic recession that prompted many Israelis to consider emigration. With dark humour, people joked that there was a sign at the airport reminding the last one to leave to turn off the lights. The prime minister now was Levi Eshkol – a wise and level-headed statesman, yet folksy and lacking charisma, making him subject to ridicule. Ben-Gurion, who had stepped down in 1963, disparaged him constantly. When Radio Cairo's Hebrew-language broadcasts started to threaten that Egypt was about "to annihilate" the State of Israel, many Israelis believed it. The word "annihilate" reminded them of the Holocaust, as they often made clear in private letters sent to relatives overseas. Various indications suggested that the Egyptians intended to carry out their threat.

The calculations of Israel's army and government were based on the assumption that the side that struck first would win and that the other would be defeated. Israel struck first, and within a few hours it destroyed the Egyptian air force while it was still on the ground. This essentially eliminated the Egyptian threat, but the sudden transition from existential panic to a near-legendary victory over the "Arab Nazis" swept the cabinet ministers into dizzying euphoria. They instructed the army to capture the Sinai up to the Suez Canal and the Gaza Strip, and, after Jordan and Syria entered the war, East Jerusalem, the West Bank and the Golan Heights.

Almost all these conquests were made without conducting a political and strategic analysis and even contradicted the views formulated about six months earlier by the heads of the Mossad, IDF military intelligence and the foreign ministry. Among these was their assessment that it would not be in Israel's interest to capture the West Bank, including East Jerusalem, because – as Zionist thought had always asserted – Israel's future as a Jewish and democratic state would be endangered by the absorption of Arab-populated territories. On the eve of the war, Moshe Dayan also believed that Israel should refrain from seizing the Gaza Strip. However, the caution expressed prior to the war gave way to a sense of exhilaration in the wake of Israel's stunning military feats, and the minutes from cabinet meetings document a growing addiction to a messianic national delusion. Almost every piece of land that was "liberated" was ascribed biblical significance. "Six Days", which became the official appellation of the war, heralded and dictated a new Genesis of sorts.

At the outbreak of the war, there were about 2.8 million people living in Israel, approximately 2.5 million of them Jews. The Six-Day War added about a million Arabs to the population, and the territory under Israeli control became 3.5 times larger. The military government in the occupied territories was cautious at first, with a declared commitment to comply strictly with international law. The extensive presence of international observers and representatives of the world media – as well as the IDF's flattering self-image as "the most moral army in the world" – engendered what the Israelis liked to describe as an "enlightened occupation", with minimal intrusion into the population's daily lives. "Foreign and military rule – the less you see and feel it, the easier it is to bear," stated the official summary of the initial three years of occupation. "The only democracy in the

> *"The only democracy in the Middle East", as Israel liked to describe itself, was still very sensitive to its image*

Middle East", as Israel liked to describe itself, was still very sensitive to its image. And when a Palestinian terrorist hid in the basement of the mayor of Gaza's home, Defence Minister Moshe Dayan acceded to a request from a member of the Elkayam family and refrained from demolishing the building, though legally empowered to do so, both in consideration of the mayor's pro-Jewish stance in 1929 and to illustrate that Israel knew how to reward those who stood with it, just as it knew how to punish its enemies.

Most Israelis were opposed to a complete withdrawal from the territories and conditioned even a partial withdrawal on peace accords with the Arabs. Indeed, the decision not to return all the captured territories to the Arabs – annexed East Jerusalem in particular – reflected a religious-nationalistic yearning, a sudden longing to impose Israeli rule over the entirety of the biblical Promised Land. This was expressed in the slogan: "What was liberated will not be returned." (In Hebrew, this rhymes.) Before long, Jewish settlements began popping up in the territories; this was ostensibly a continuation of the Zionist settlement project that began in the nineteenth century, but was in fact contrary to the Zionist principle of separation. The question was what to do with the Palestinians. Most Israelis never recognised their state's role in creating the human tragedy of the Nakba refugees and never gave much thought to the national and communal identity of those refugees. Prime Minister Eshkol and his successor, Golda Meir, regarded them, and the population of Gaza in particular, as a demographic, economic and security problem. There were also some Israelis who warned that this issue was a ticking bomb.

There was a feeling in Israel that it was crucial to reduce the number of refugees in Gaza. This inspired a number of concrete plans, including one to transfer 250,000 refugees to the West Bank and to propose that Jordan absorb them, together with the West Bank, within the framework of a peace accord. There were also plans to settle them in the West Bank even if Jordan proved unwilling to receive them. But a number of ministers in Eshkol's governing coalition believed that the lands of the West Bank should be kept for Jewish settlement. Meanwhile, Eshkol recalled a Zionist plan from the 1930s to transfer the Arabs of Palestine to Iraq and decided to explore the possibility of transferring Palestinian refugees from Gaza to other countries.

In early 1968, a five-person team began to work in the prime minister's office on a secret operation. Their role was to convince the Arabs to leave Gaza in exchange for a payment that would cover the cost of moving to Jordan and their initial needs there. The woman appointed to coordinate the operation, Ada Sereni, was a heroic figure in the history of the Zionist project, noted for her participation in various clandestine operations, mainly involving immigration of Holocaust survivors. Eshkol hoped her connections in Italy, where she was born, might help facilitate the emigration of Arabs from Gaza to Libya, a former Italian colony. Sereni believed that within two years it would be possible to evacuate 40,000 families from Gaza, a total of about 250,000 people,

The operation undermined the flattering self-image of some Israelis and stirred condemnation overseas

and estimated that US$10 million would be needed to finance the operation. "I'd like all of them to leave, even if it is to the moon," the prime minister told her. He kept close track of the operation and met with Sereni once a week, greeting her each time by asking: "How many Arabs did you send off today?"

In mid-May 1968, Sereni reported to Eshkol that during the first three months of her work, about 15,000 people had left Gaza for Jordan. However, Eshkol felt that the project was turning out to be too costly and many thousands of Gazans left without receiving payment. It seems that illicit means of spurring emigration were also considered, including the purchase of 1000 passports from an interior minister of a South American country. In one of the discussions on how to accelerate the evacuation of Gaza, the suggestion was made to disrupt the supply of food to the city. In addition, US senator Edward Kennedy was pursuing a plan to send 200,000 refugees from Gaza to various countries throughout the world, designating up to 50,000 of them for absorption in the United States.

Nevertheless, most of the Palestinians remained in Gaza and became a key component in the conflict over Israel-Palestine. During the year that followed the 1967 war, 687 acts of terror and border incidents were recorded. One hundred and seventy-five Israelis were killed – including ten civilians, and over 500 were injured, including eighty-five civilians. Some of the perpetrators came from Gaza, whose population now totalled about 400,000 people, of which 80 per cent were Nakba refugees or their children.

In early January 1971, a grenade was tossed into the car of an Israeli family on a weekend outing not far from Gaza, killing a ten-year-old boy and his five-year-old sister and severely injuring their mother. The murderer was a Palestinian teenager, fifteen-and-a-half years old, from the second generation of the Nakba. The murder shook Israel and marked the end of the "enlightened occupation". Major General Ariel Sharon, the head of the IDF's Northern Command and later prime minister, orchestrated a major operation to suppress the terror cells in Gaza and its environs. Over 100 Palestinians were killed and more than 700 were injured. The operation undermined the flattering self-image of some Israelis and stirred condemnation overseas. Yet the world (like most Israelis) did not show any special interest in the refugees, with the exception of an annual UN report and assistance provided by the organisation.

Some Israelis continued to visit the markets in Gaza and eat at its fish restaurants, and labourers from Gaza started working in Israel. By the 1970s, an effort was underway to integrate Gaza into an ambitious development project and populate northern Gaza with Israelis. As part of the project, a new Israeli city, Yamit, was built. Plans were drafted for new residential neighbourhoods for Palestinians in the Gaza Strip. Those opting to live in these neighbourhoods would forfeit their status as refugees entitled to UN support. Few of the refugees found this option attractive.

14. Deals and disengagement

Slowly, apparently insulted to the depths of his soul, he asked: "So am I Nebuchadnezzar?"

After the Yom Kippur War, which surprised Israel in October 1973, and the Camp David talks, which culminated in a peace treaty between Israel and Egypt in September 1979, the two states agreed that Gaza and the West Bank would be granted autonomy, to come into effect within five years. After signing the treaty, which was brokered by US president Jimmy Carter and which mandated Israel's withdrawal from Sinai, President Anwar Sadat and Prime Minister Menachem Begin were awarded the Nobel Peace Prize. Meanwhile, no one could accuse Begin of surrendering part of the Land of Israel, since Sinai lay outside its borders. The successor to Jabotinsky, Begin was a classic European liberal nationalist, committed not only to the "complete homeland" but also to human liberty, national security and the supremacy of the law. He often warned that a prolonged occupation could turn Israel into something akin to Rhodesia. (Due to Israel's important relations with South Africa, Begin refrained from mentioning that country in this context – except in closed cabinet meetings.) When referring to the Palestinians, he would say with theatrical emphasis "*Paleshtinaim*" to identity them as descendants of the Philistines – pronounced *Pleeshtim* in Hebrew. In this vein, some have found a possible connection between the name of the Philistines and the Hebrew word for invader, *polesh*.

The Palestinians, who were not partners in the Camp David Accords, wanted exactly what Begin wanted when he was in a comparable situation under British rule – an independent state. The autonomy plan for Gaza and the West Bank was thus consigned to oblivion, together with countless other ideas, proposals and plans for resolving the conflict. The simplest solution of all was suggested by one of the leaders of the Labor Party, Abraham Katz-Oz from Kibbutz Nahal Oz: to return the Gaza Strip to Egypt. His proposal sparked a debate in his party that was conducted, as usual in Israel, without considering what might be acceptable to the Arabs themselves. President Sadat, who wisely recoiled from taking on the hornets' nest of Gaza and the refugees, was assassinated in 1981 by Islamic extremists.

Between 1993 and 1995, Prime Minister Yitzhak Rabin and Foreign Minister Shimon Peres signed the Oslo Accords with the PLO, which entailed relinquishing Gaza and part of the West Bank, and they too received the Nobel Peace Prize, alongside Yasser Arafat. The aftermath of the Oslo Accords underscored the impact of internal discord among the Israelis and Palestinians, with rival groups on both sides claiming to represent the genuine sentiments of the peoples, the imperative of history, or even a divine mission. The accords ushered in a wave of terrorism sparked by the murder of dozens of Muslim worshippers by an Israeli settler in Hebron. About a year and a half later, Rabin was assassinated by an Israeli right-wing extremist who opposed, among other things, the territorial concession of Gaza. The Palestinians also engaged in internecine battles and most people on both sides shifted rightwards in their views, towards the unhinged realms of patriotism and nationalism.

Israel revised its policies vis-à-vis Gaza from time to time: The stronger the Palestinian national movement grew in the territories and the more international recognition it garnered, the more inclined Israel became to separate the West Bank from the Gaza Strip with the aim of preventing the possibility of a Palestinian state. A long and bloody series of Palestinian acts of terror and rebellion led to Prime Minister Sharon's decision in 2005 to dismantle Israel's seventeen Gush Katif settlements in the southern Gaza Strip, along with three Jewish settlements in the northern Gaza Strip and four in the northern West Bank. Most of the settlements in Gaza had been built in the 1970s and 1980s and were home to about 8000 Jewish Israelis. They comprised less than 1 per cent of the population of the Gaza Strip, but controlled about a quarter of its territory. The homes were attractive, with their red roofs and flower gardens, radiating a warm welcome. But the residents' daily lives were beleaguered by non-stop attacks by Palestinian organisations, sometimes with mortar fire and rockets. Sharon was a military man and the "disengagement", as it was called, was designed to reduce the defence burden on the Gaza front and strengthen Israel's control in the West Bank. In the history of the Zionist project, it was a singularly provocative decision. Though the disengagement won parliamentary approval, it significantly deepened the ideological and emotional rift in Israeli society.

Gaza had only once in a thousand years been the epicentre of a spiritual upheaval in the Jewish world. Otherwise, it had never attracted more than a few dozen Jewish families or developed a particularly glorious tradition to hand down from generation to generation. Now, however, Gaza was forcing Israelis to undergo an agonising process of questioning their collective and personal identities and re-examining the very basis of national existence in the Land of Israel.

Most television broadcasters adopted the thesis that the evacuation of Jewish settlers from the Gaza Strip was a national disaster and was "painful for all of us". They spoke in the language of the settlers – "uprooting", "expulsion" and "trauma". The settlers were described again and again as "wonderful people", agents of true Zionist patriotism. Some of the settlers announced that they would not leave their homes voluntarily but would refrain from forcibly resisting the soldiers and police officers sent to evacuate them. Many of them believed in their ability to convince these security forces of the historical, national and personal justice of their cause and thus, at the last minute, deter them from carrying out their orders. The settlers rehearsed emotional manipulation and the security forces were trained to withstand it.

Several dozen Border Patrol soldiers lined up along the path leading to the synagogue in the Morag settlement. The soldiers, most in their early twenties, had been instructed not to engage in confrontations with the settlers. A seventeen-year-old settler with a beautiful face, in the flower of her youth, approached one of them. She drew close and provoked him with the usual words: "Look me in the eyes," she asked. "What will you tell your children one day? Think about your mother." The young man, no more than two years older than the girl and a little taller, tried to focus above her head, as if gazing at the flag at an official state ceremony. The young woman did not relent. He turned his head away from her and covered his mouth with his

The disengagement was recognised as a national trauma

hand. She moved closer until she was almost touching him and silently flashed a sweet and seductive smile; it was almost an erotic provocation. The young man kept his composure and, luckily, his commander came to relieve him.

At another settlement, Neve Dekalim, several soldiers and a junior officer, a lieutenant, stood at the entrance to a home. A group of boys and girls were skipping and dancing around them, reciting names and phrases from Jewish history: Abraham our forefather, Moses our teacher, King David, the Temple, Nebuchadnezzar, the expulsion from Spain, Eichmann, Hitler. One of the soldiers could no longer restrain himself: "What are you comparing to the

Holocaust?" He blurted something about the obligation to obey the decisions of the majority in a democracy. A brief argument ensued as if they were in history class. One of the commanders hurried to muzzle the soldier and shooed him away. He now stood on the side, alone, a rosy-cheeked lad, bespectacled, who looked like he was probably a good student. He bit his lips and was clearly struggling to restrain himself. Very quietly, in a deep voice, slowly, apparently insulted to the depths of his soul, he asked: "So am I Nebuchadnezzar?" An officer, taller than him, came and moved him further away.

The disengagement was recognised as a national trauma. Within a year, a centre was established to "commemorate the heritage" of Gush Katif. A law was later passed that accorded the centre a status similar to that of the state's official Holocaust remembrance institution, Yad Vashem. The Gush Katif Heritage Center includes a special museum and a collection of recorded testimonies from settlers, and runs a range of educational programmes. The centre also helped to publish Haggai Huberman's book on the history of the Jewish community in Gaza, which describes the dismantling of settlements as a religious-national tragedy reminiscent of the destruction of the Temple: "That night, all the synagogues of the Gaza Strip communities were ablaze," Huberman wrote. "The Palestinian rioters stormed the empty buildings and excitedly set them on fire. All of them went up in flames ... the image of the red flames against the backdrop of the black night will forever remain one of the images that symbolised, more than anything, the destruction of Jewish settlement of the

[Gaza] Strip." Faithful to the tradition of Jewish belief, Huberman did not lose hope. "I believe with complete faith that the synagogues will be rebuilt and arise in their full glory at their original site in the Gaza Strip," he wrote, adding an expression of faith and political intent: "May it be rebuilt and established speedily in our days. Amen".

15. October 7

The war that started in 2023 came more than 2000 years after Alexander Yannai, the Hasmonean king, ordered the destruction of Gaza.

In 2006, elections were held in the Palestinian territories and were won by the Hamas organisation, which seized control of Gaza in 2007. Besides instituting a tyrannical Islamic regime, the organisation almost immediately began launching attacks on Israeli communities, using weapons such as incendiary balloons, rockets and missiles, some of them homemade. Israel and Egypt imposed various restrictions on Gaza – on entry and exit, and on the regular supply of water, fuel, electricity, food and medical equipment. The unemployment rate soared to 50 per cent. "The scandal is expressed in Israel's success in incarcerating 2 million residents of the Strip, most of them 1948 refugees, and marginalising them by turning them into what looks more and more like a giant collection of beggars," wrote Amira Hass in *Haaretz*. Hass was very familiar with the situation in Gaza and even lived there for a while. "When Palestinian suffering will be completely different, much worse," the author A.B. Yehoshua wrote, "they themselves will wipe out the terror." In reality, the opposite occurred. Hamas expanded, deepened and enhanced a network of tunnels built earlier for smuggling, using them to move its forces and to store military equipment, including missiles.

From time to time, Israel deployed its army against the Gaza Strip, conducting aerial bombings and punitive operations that became increasingly brutal over the years. Paradoxically, at the same time Israel propped up the regime in Gaza as a way of deepening the divide between the Palestinian Authority and Hamas, in keeping with the doctrine of "divide and conquer". Accordingly, Israel facilitated Qatar's transfer of suitcases full of cash to Gaza, some of which was used to boost the organisation's array of missiles and other military capabilities. This policy reflected a conception identified with Prime Minister Benjamin Netanyahu, who has now served in his role longer than any of his predecessors. Gaza became "a demographic, security and political powder keg, tied to Israel in a Gordian knot dipped in blood, a place with no future, a problem with no solution, a thorn in the butt", to quote an article that appeared in *Haaretz* five years before the massacre of October 7, 2023.

It was the fiftieth anniversary of the Yom Kippur War, which until then was seen as the worst blow the Arabs had inflicted on Israel since its founding. Motorised Hamas forces easily breached the border fence and unleashed a rampage of murder and destruction in a number of Israeli communities that referred to themselves by the pastoral nickname "Gaza Envelope". The site of the Nova music festival, where a large crowd of revellers had gathered for an all-night rave, became a killing field. It was the most brutal terror attack Israel had ever known. Hamas may have sensed that political discord in Israel had not only sapped the strength of its society but had also undermined its military might. In any case, about 1200 Israelis were killed, most of them civilians, and several hundred were taken hostage; the atrocities included sexual violence. In the initial hours, the Hamas attackers encountered very little resistance. Israel was paralysed with shock – not only at the scope of the bestial massacre, but at the way regional security needs had been neglected and at the subsequent failures of rescue efforts.

It seemed that the trauma of the massacre was eclipsing the memory of the Holocaust

Prime Minister Netanyahu described Hamas as "Arab Nazis" and some spoke of the "October 7 Holocaust". In the following months, it seemed that the trauma of the massacre was eclipsing the memory of the Holocaust. Photographs documenting the Hamas attack in Kibbutz Kfar Aza and the murder of over sixty people were exhibited at the Jerusalem Theatre under the title "Holocaust at the Kibbutz". The national angst, pain and humiliation focused on the hostages.

During the ensuing war, the Palestinians showered missiles upon Israeli's cities and completely disrupted everyday life. In the shadow of war, about a quarter of a million Israelis were forced to evacuate their homes in the Gaza Envelope and near the border with Lebanon. Hundreds of Israeli soldiers were killed. Israel responded with an aerial attack. But what initially appeared to be a punitive response and a campaign of vengeance against specific Hamas targets soon devolved into mass expulsions within Gaza and bombardments that seemed designed to lay waste to the entire enclave, not sparing its hospitals, schools or food distribution centres. Tens of thousands of Palestinian civilians were killed, among them at least 10,000 children. The number of Palestinians killed was greater than in all the previous years of conflict combined, including the Nakba of 1948.

Israeli TV broadcasts rarely showed any horrific images of the humanitarian catastrophe in Gaza and mainly referred to it in the context of reports on the international outcry over Israel's actions. Most Israelis were inclined to see this criticism as an expression of antisemitism. Several months passed before *Haaretz* gradually began to share with its readers pictures and reports of what was happening in Gaza. About a year and a half into the war, *Haaretz* correspondent Nir Hasson wrote: "We have entered the monstrous stage." Some foreign observers, including Jean-Pierre Filiu, a French expert on Gaza, provided detailed accounts of the catastrophe, describing the food shortages, lack of drinking water and collapse of the medical system. Pictures of starving Palestinian children appeared on the front pages of newspapers around the world. Hundreds of thousands of Israelis demonstrated for more urgent action to win the hostages' release, but if they felt shame or even guilt about what was being done in their name in Gaza, most remained silent.

In the history of relations between Gaza and Jews, there have been signs of grace here and there, such as a "sister cities" agreement once signed between Gaza and Tel Aviv, and a prayer for peace in Gaza and for the health of its residents that appears in a new book edited by the historian Dotan Halevy. The prayer, which resonates with the rhymes of the liturgical poet Israel Najara, was composed by Omri Ben Yehuda and published some six months before the Hamas invasion. And there are others. About a year-and-a-half into the war, an elderly demonstrator, who had apparently not lost his faith in goodness, stood on a street in Jerusalem's upscale Rehavia neighbourhood, holding a sign that called for an immediate end to the fighting: "Now". Two security guards approached and asked him to move away, so as not to disturb the neighbours. The incident occurred on Aza Street. Its name, which dates back to the British mandate, is the Hebrew for "Gaza". One of its residents is Benjamin Netanyahu.

The war that started in 2023 came more than 2000 years after Alexander Yannai, the Hasmonean king, ordered the destruction of Gaza. Since then, the city has been rebuilt and destroyed again time after time. This latest war was not primarily prosecuted with the aim of achieving defined strategic objectives. Rather, it symbolised more than anything the irrational nature of the Israeli–Palestinian conflict. There was no rational explanation for Hamas's readiness to sacrifice tens of thousands of its people to the delusion that the Jewish State of Israel will vanish from the face of the earth and give way to an Islamist state. There was also no rational explanation for Prime Minister Netanyahu's readiness to kill tens of thousands of Palestinian civilians in pursuit of a "total victory"; no one knows exactly what this meant, except perhaps the fulfilment of Ben-Gurion's dream that Gaza will be swallowed up by the sea. More than a century has passed since Ben-Gurion determined that the Israeli–Palestinian conflict defied resolution and could at best be managed, yet the conflict over Gaza was never managed more catastrophically than in the days of Hamas and Benjamin Netanyahu. ▤

Never miss an issue.
Subscribe and save.

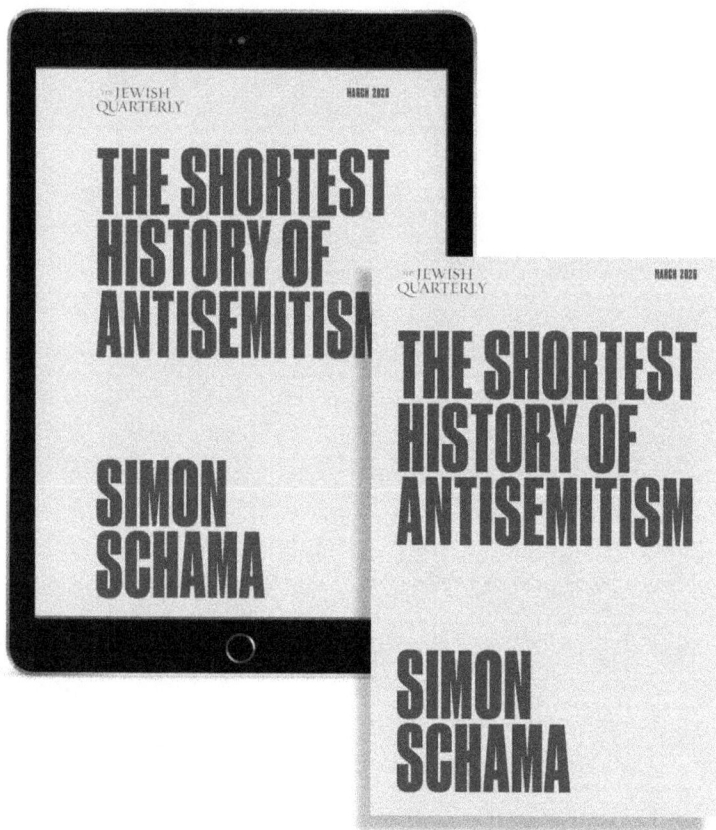

Subscribe now

- 1 year print and digital subscription (4 issues)
  £42 GBP | $56 USD | $74.99 AUD
- 1 year digital subscription (4 issues)
  £25 GBP | $32 USD | $44.99 AUD

Visit **jewishquarterly.com/subscribe**
Email **subscribe@jewishquarterly.com**

Or scan the QR code with your mobile device camera:

PART OF AN INSTITUTION? RECOMMEND JQ TO YOUR LIBRARY.
An institutional digital subscription provides students, academics and staff with access to more than 70 years of back issues, as well as each new issue as it is published. Visit our subscribe page or send us an email to learn more.

PRICES INCLUDE POSTAGE AND HANDLING.
Prices and discounts current at the time of printing. Your subscription will automatically renew until you notify us to stop. We will send you a reminder notice prior to the end of your subscription period.

www.ingramcontent.com/pod-product-compliance
Lightning Source LLC
Chambersburg PA
CBHW021150090426
42740CB00008B/1026